SIMPLE MAZES FOR CHILDREN

75 Mazes with Five Levels of Difficulty for Kids

written by

Peter I. Kattan
and
Nicola I. Kattan

www.PetraBooks.com

www.PetraBooks.com

Ordering Information:
Quantity sales. Special discounts are available on quantity purchases by corporations, associations. Orders by U.S. trade bookstores and wholesalers. Please visit www.PetraBooks.com

Printed in the United States of America

ISBN-979-8-8691-9957-7

1
SUPER EASY

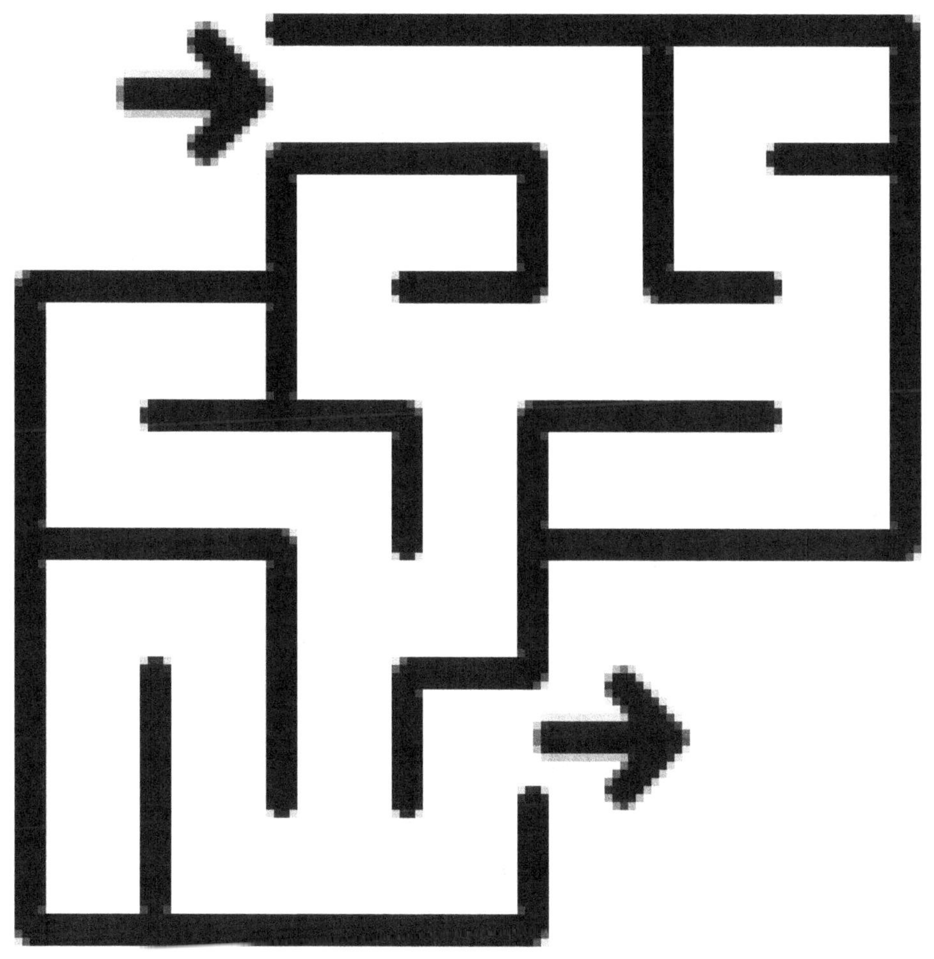

2
SUPER EASY

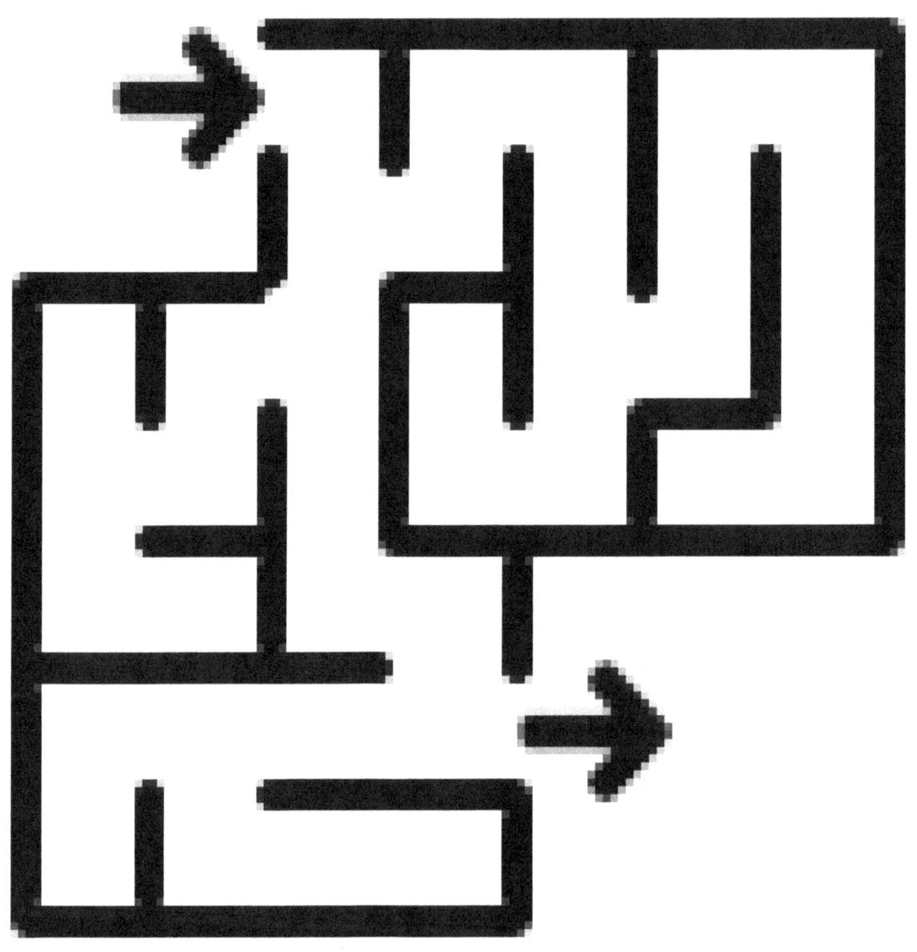

3
SUPER EASY

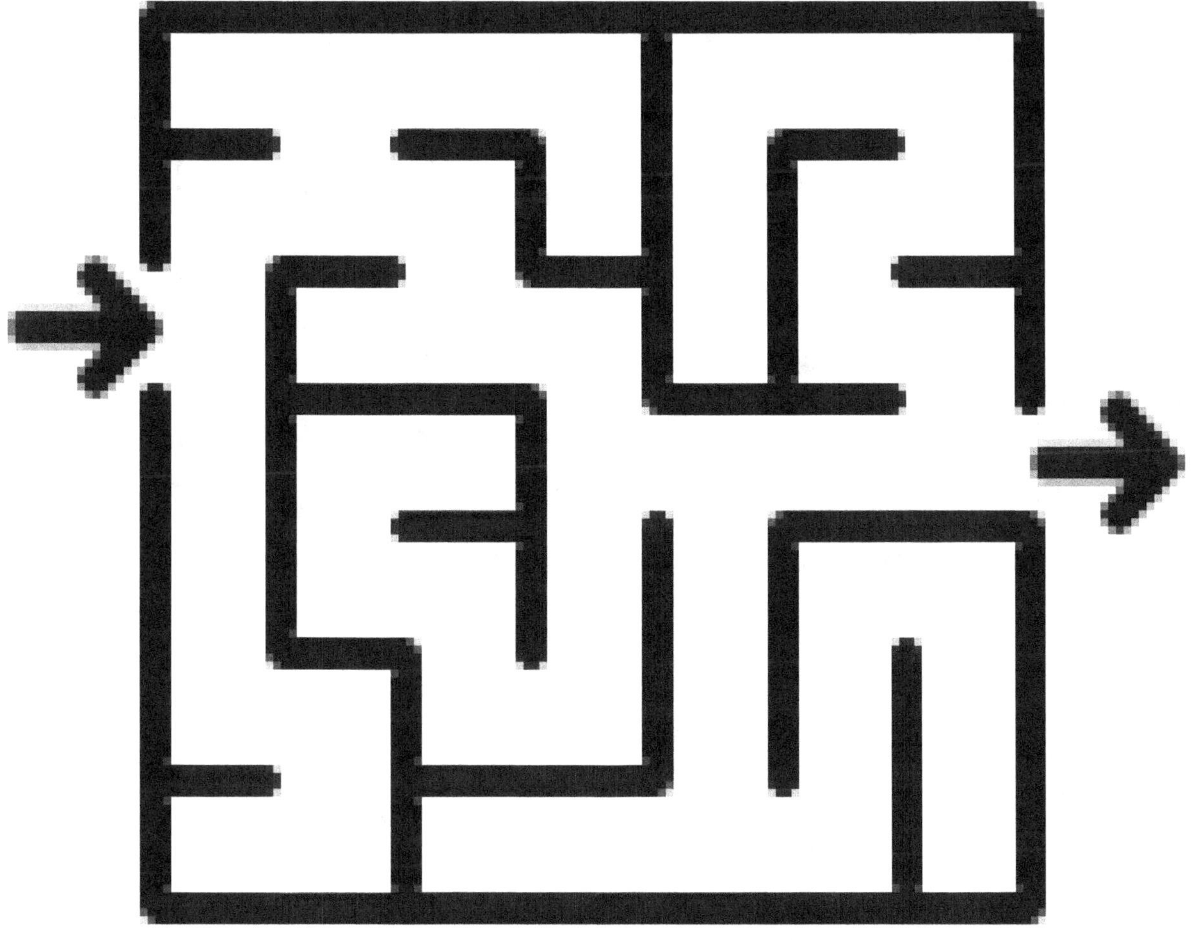

4
SUPER EASY

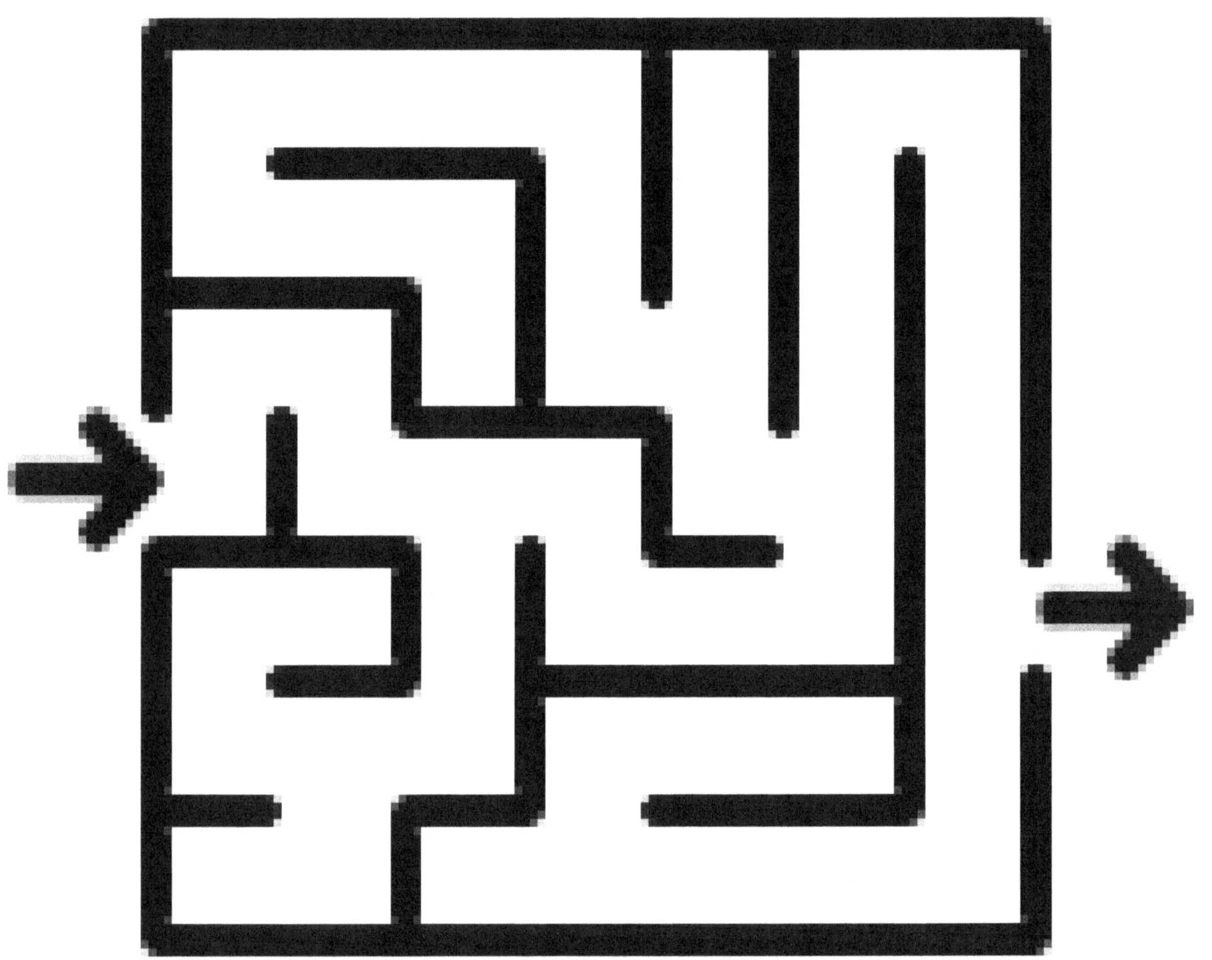

5
SUPER EASY

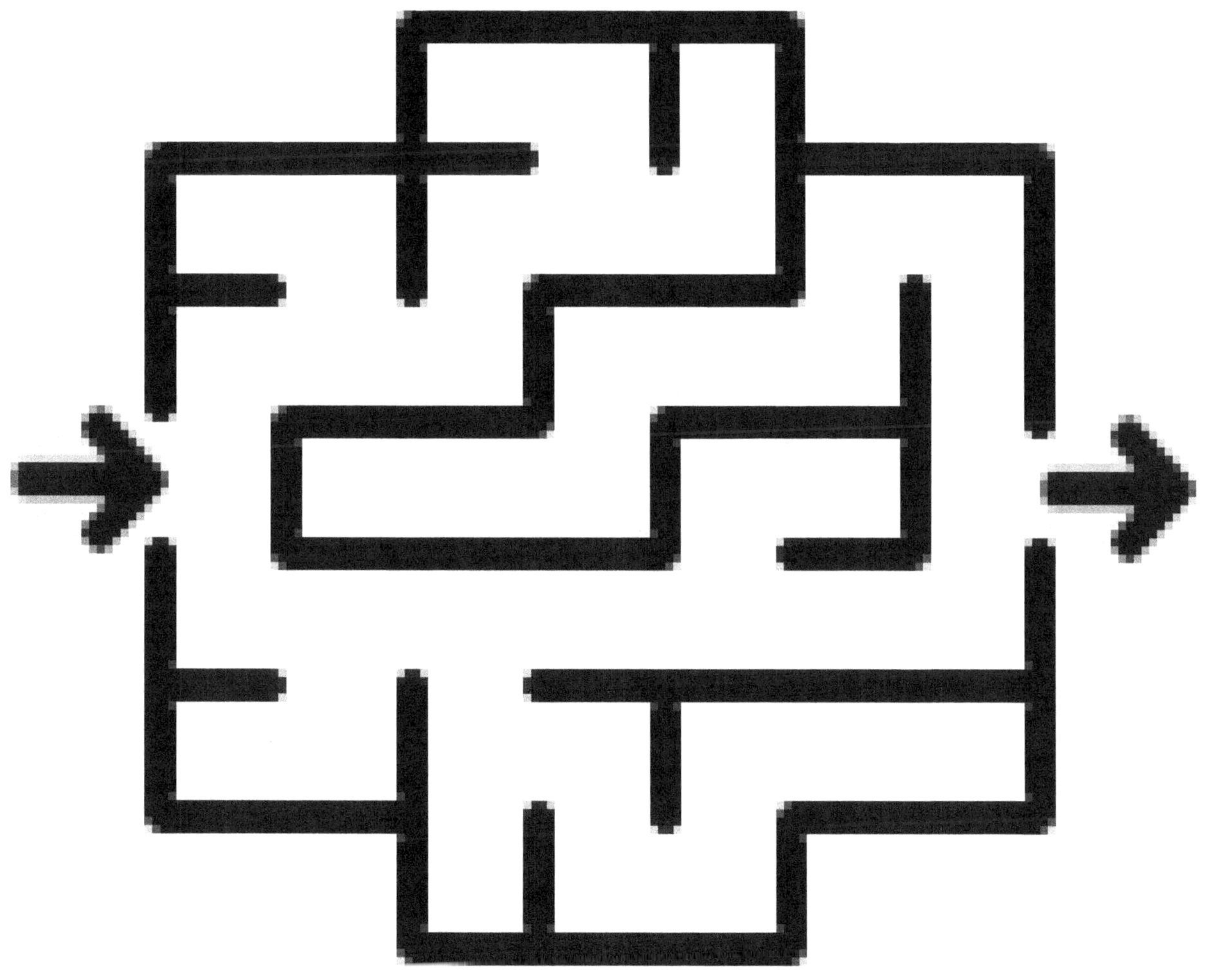

6
SUPER EASY

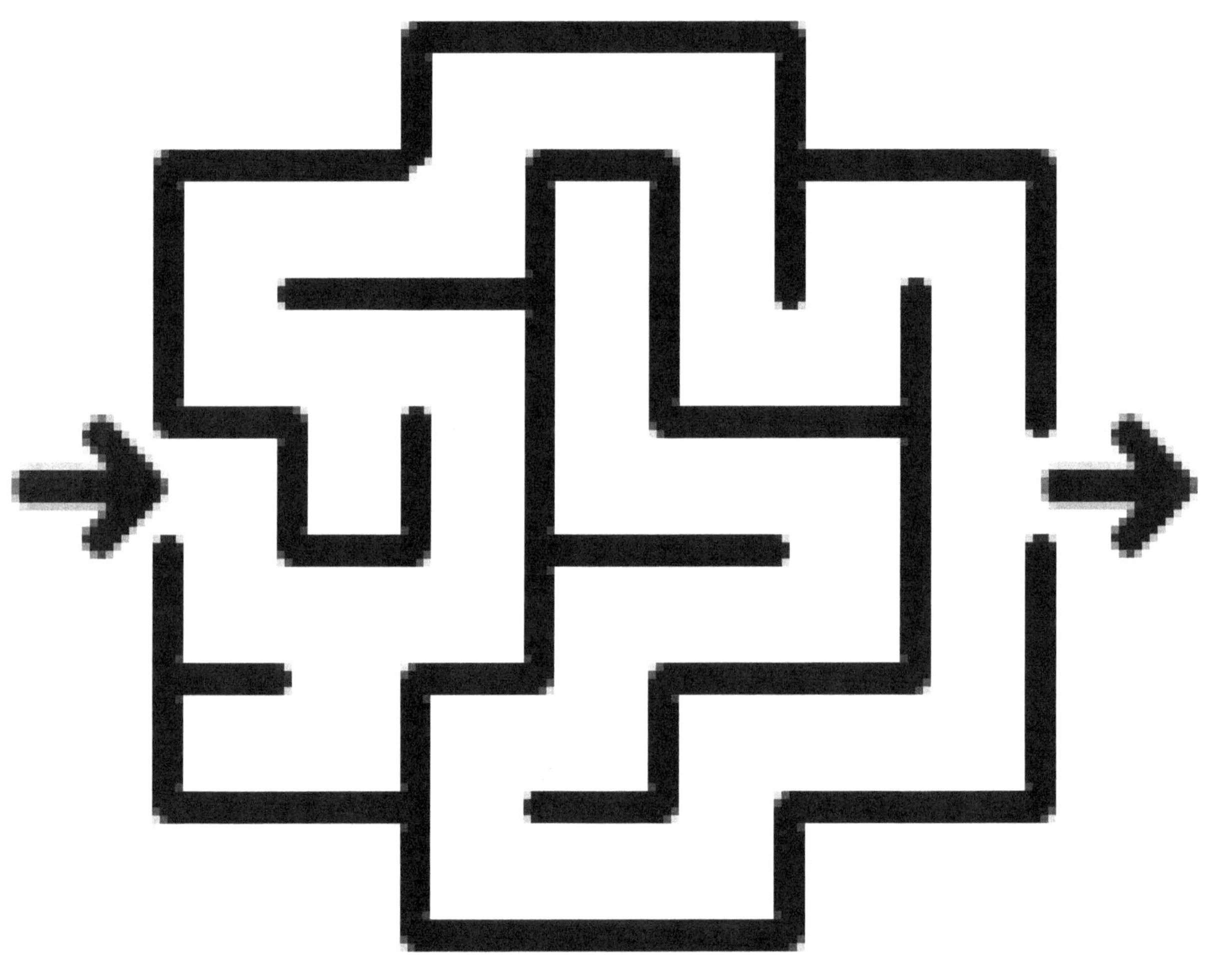

7
SUPER EASY

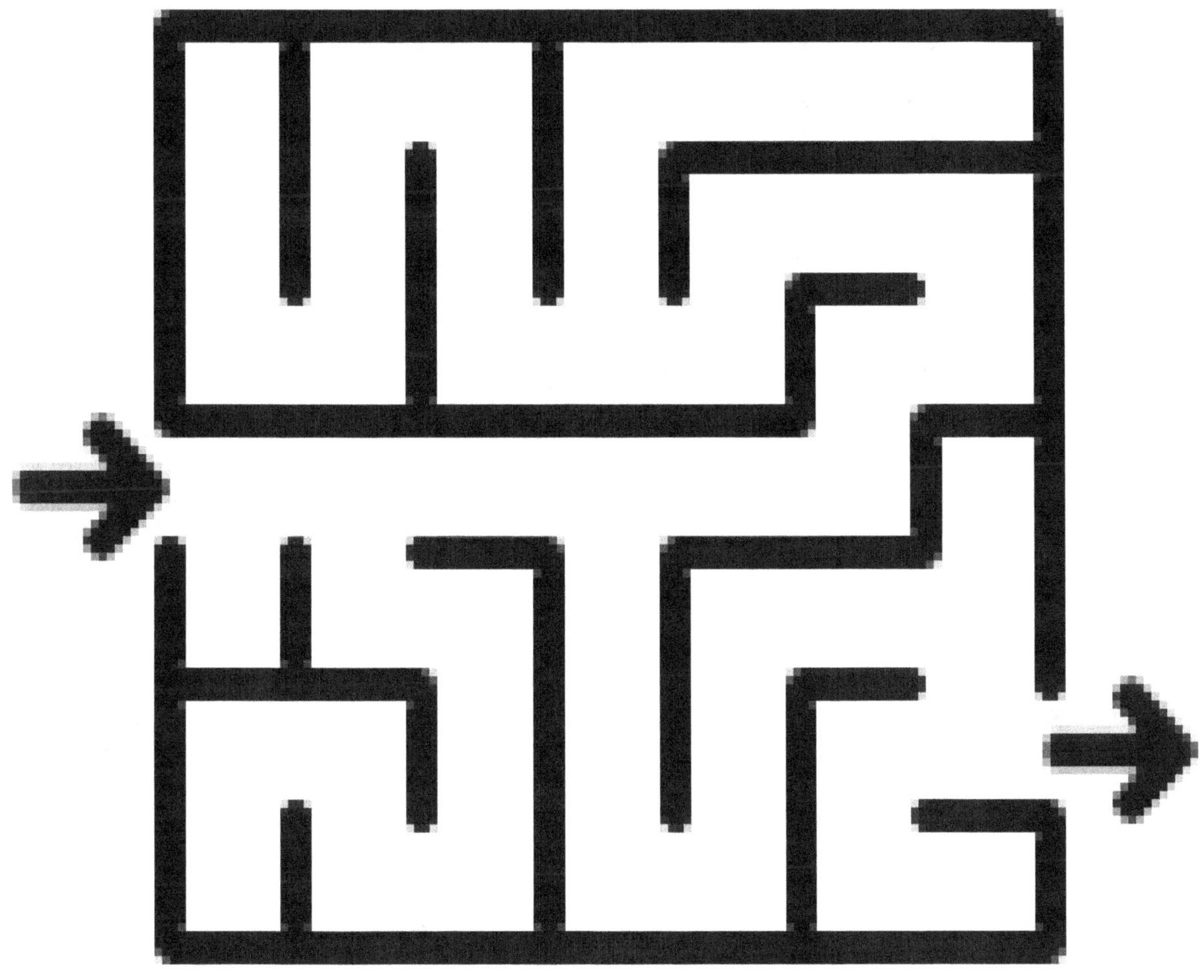

8
SUPER EASY

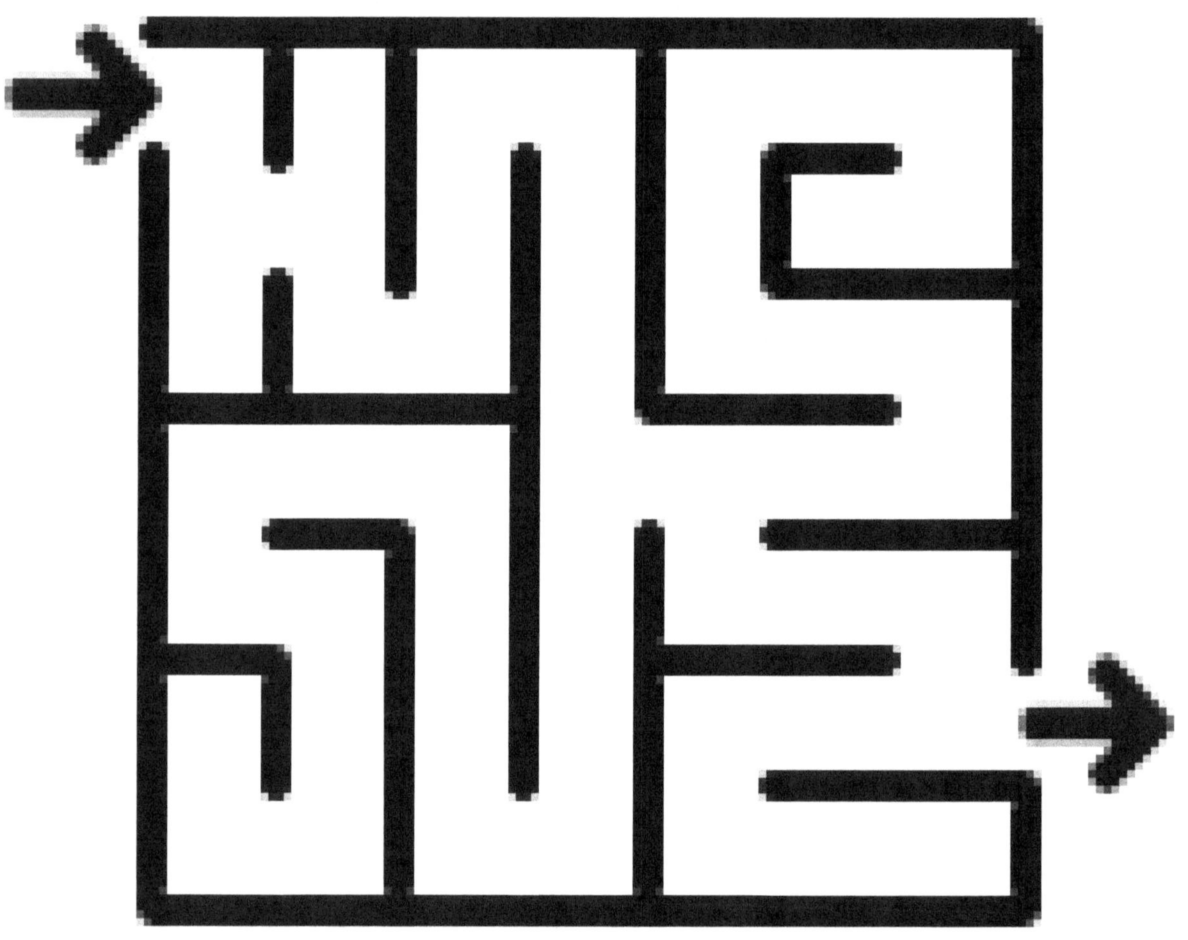

9
SUPER EASY

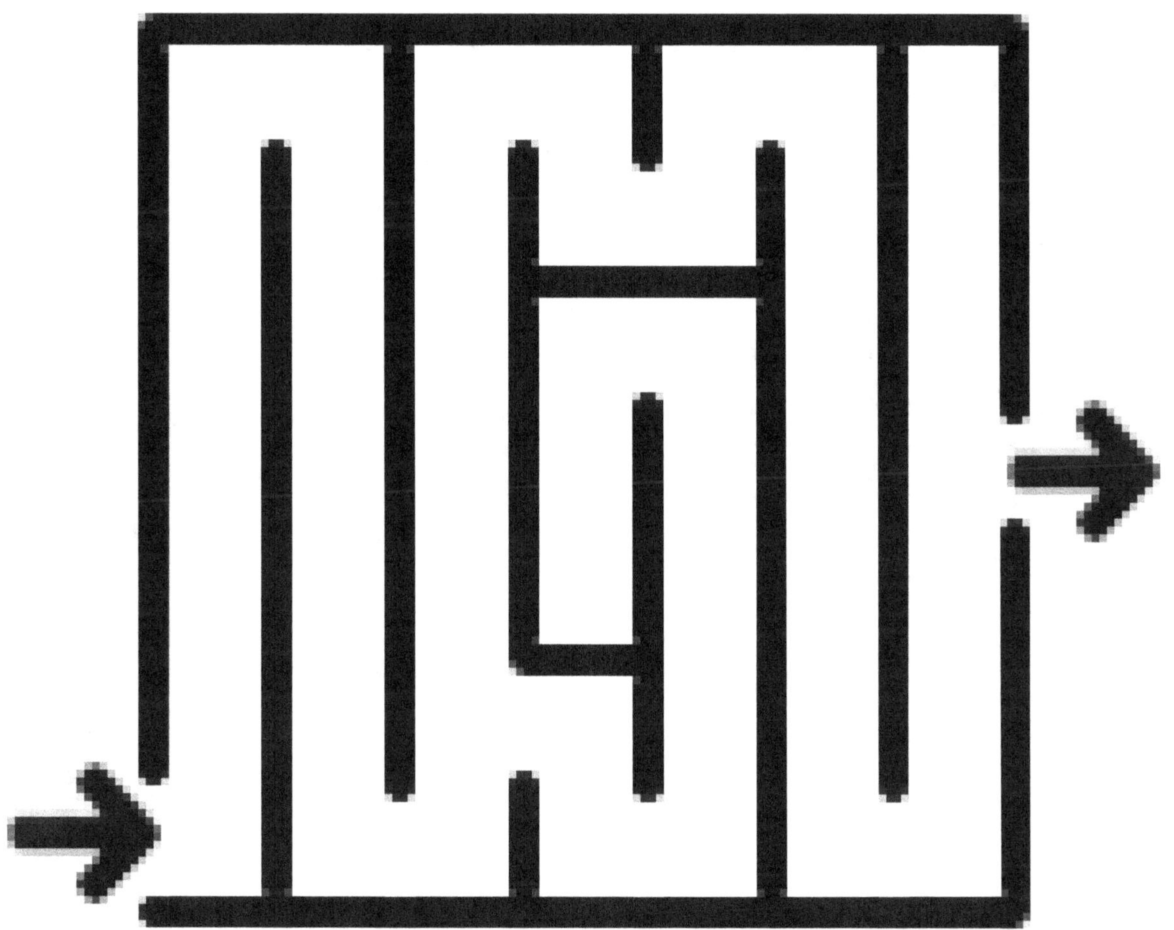

10
SUPER EASY

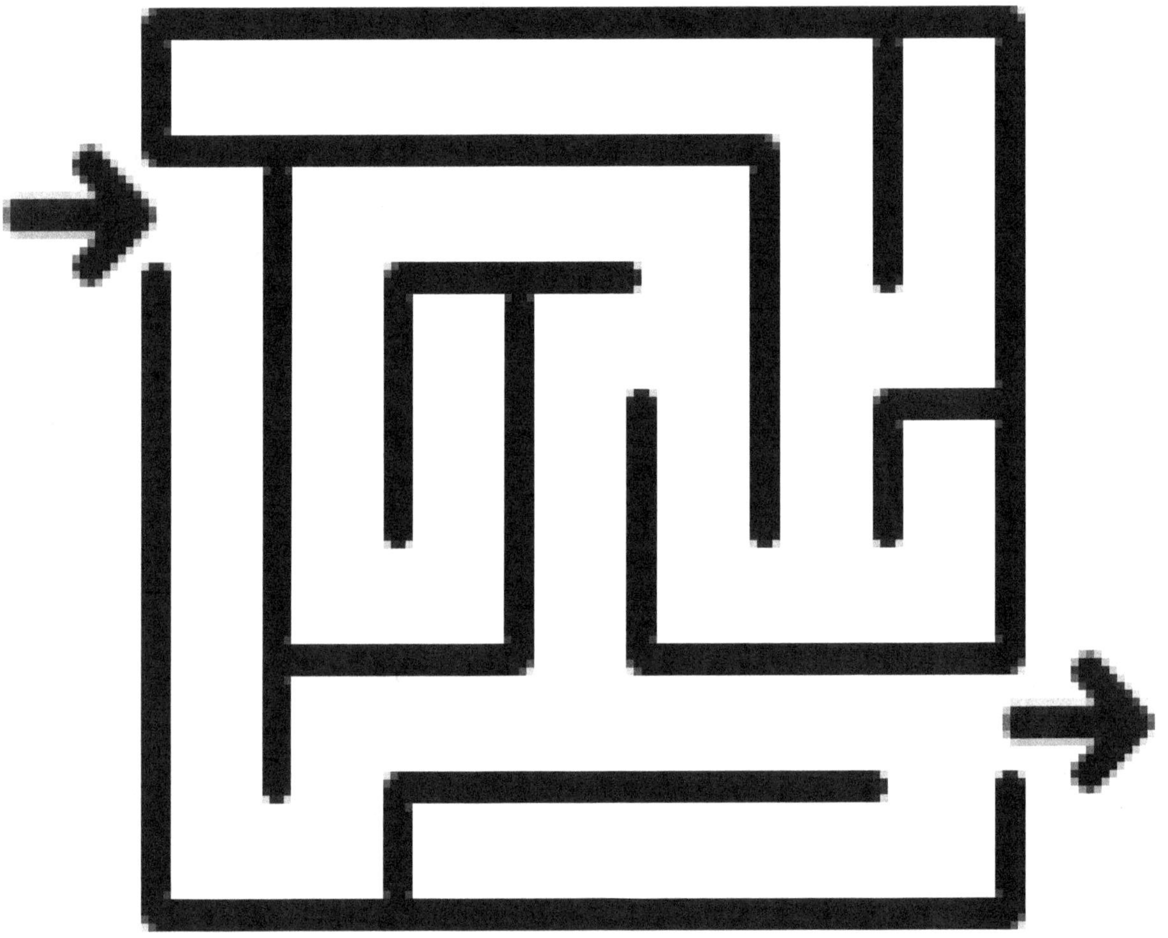

11
SUPER EASY

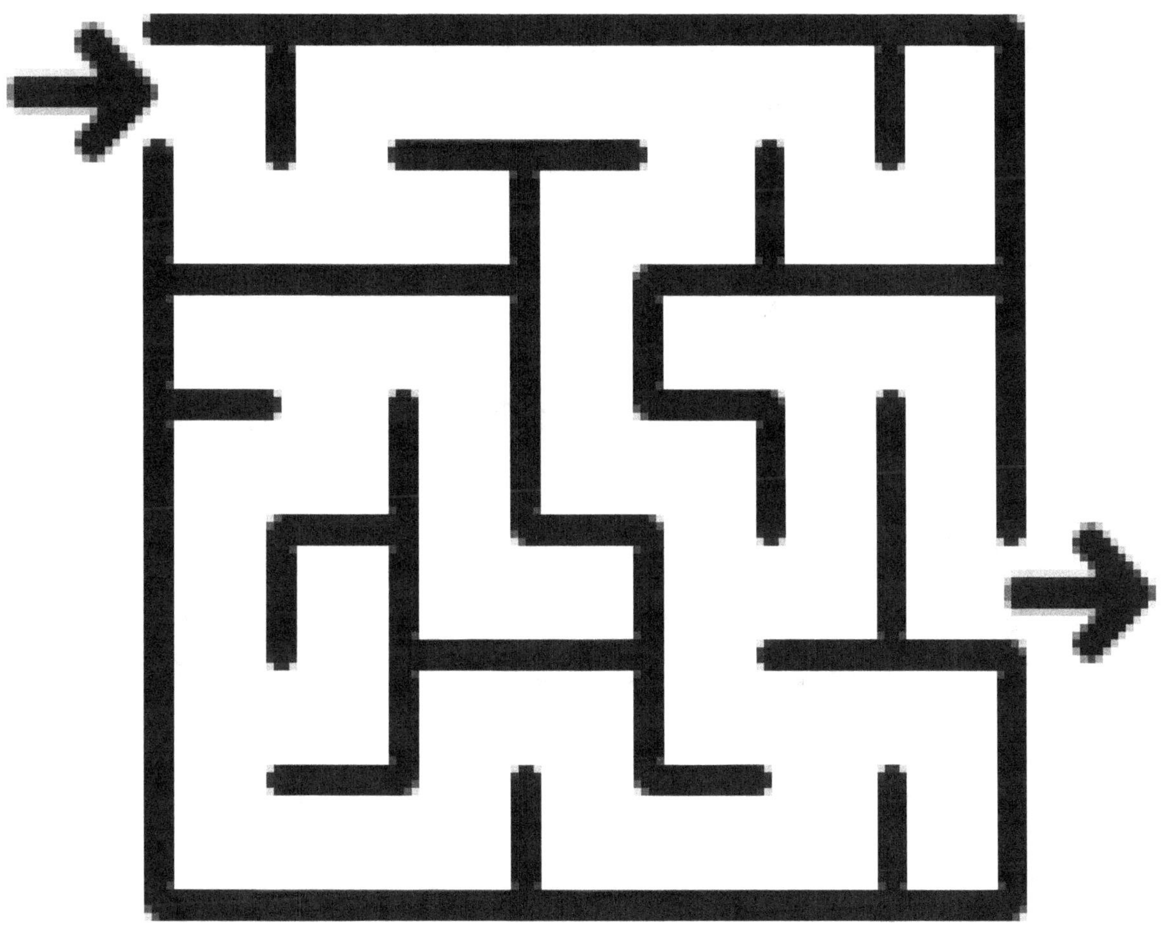

12
SUPER EASY

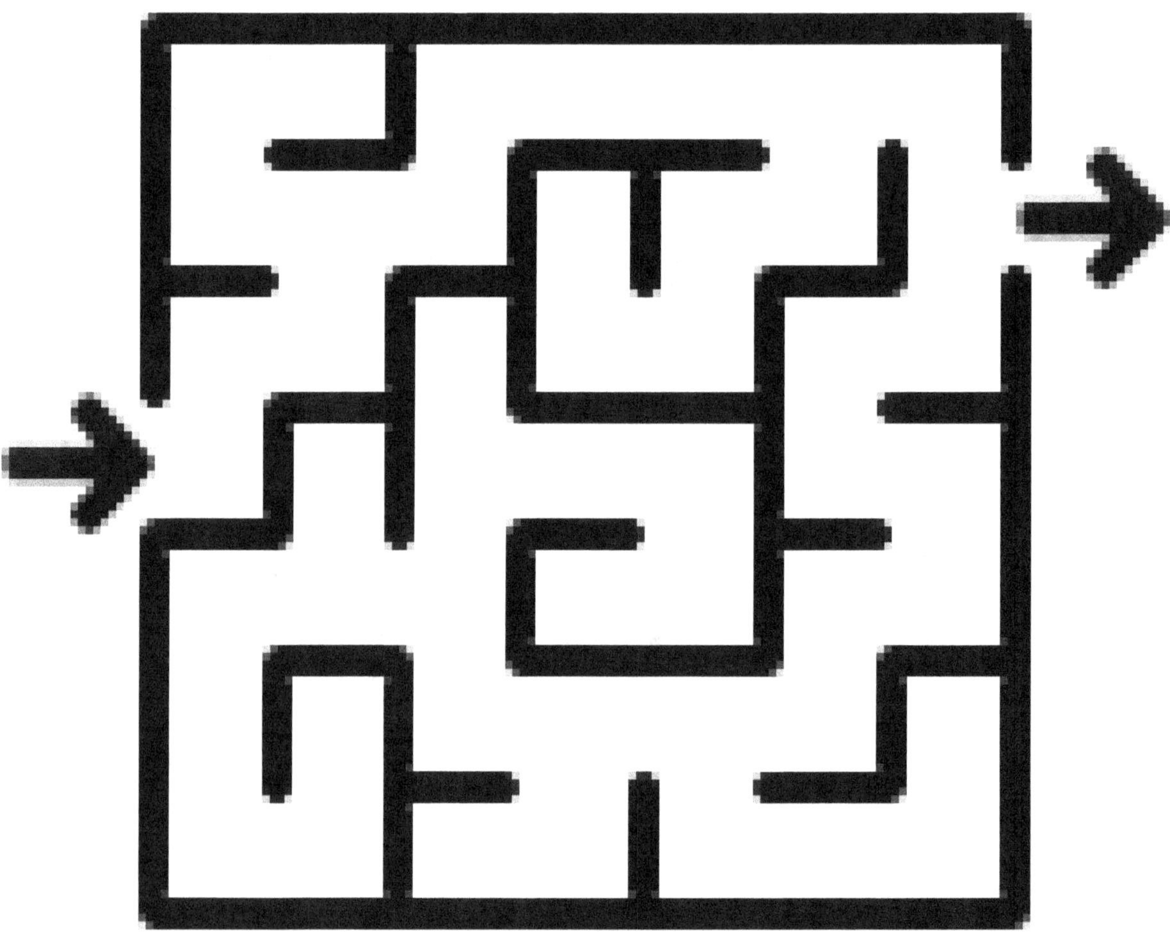

13
SUPER EASY

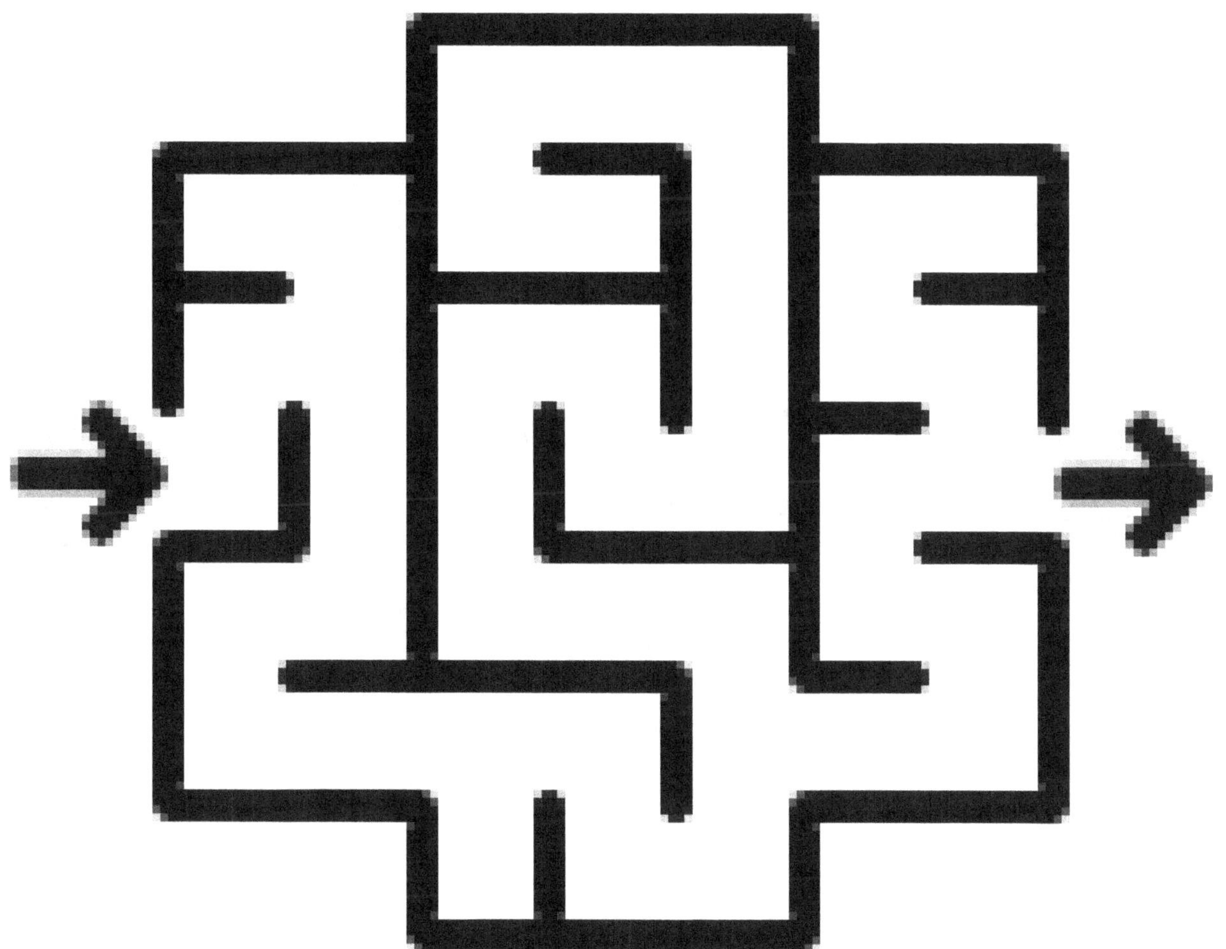

14
SUPER EASY

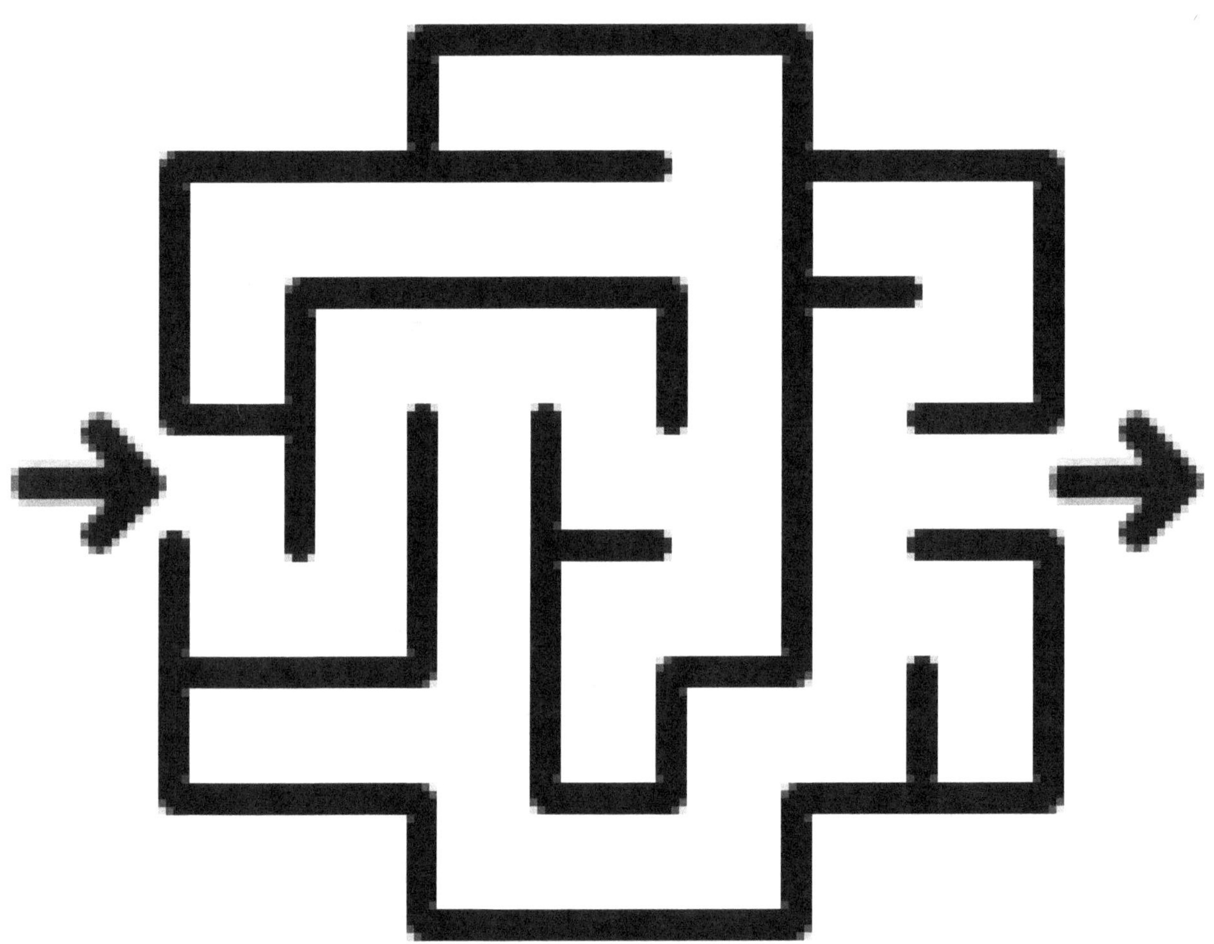

15
SUPER EASY

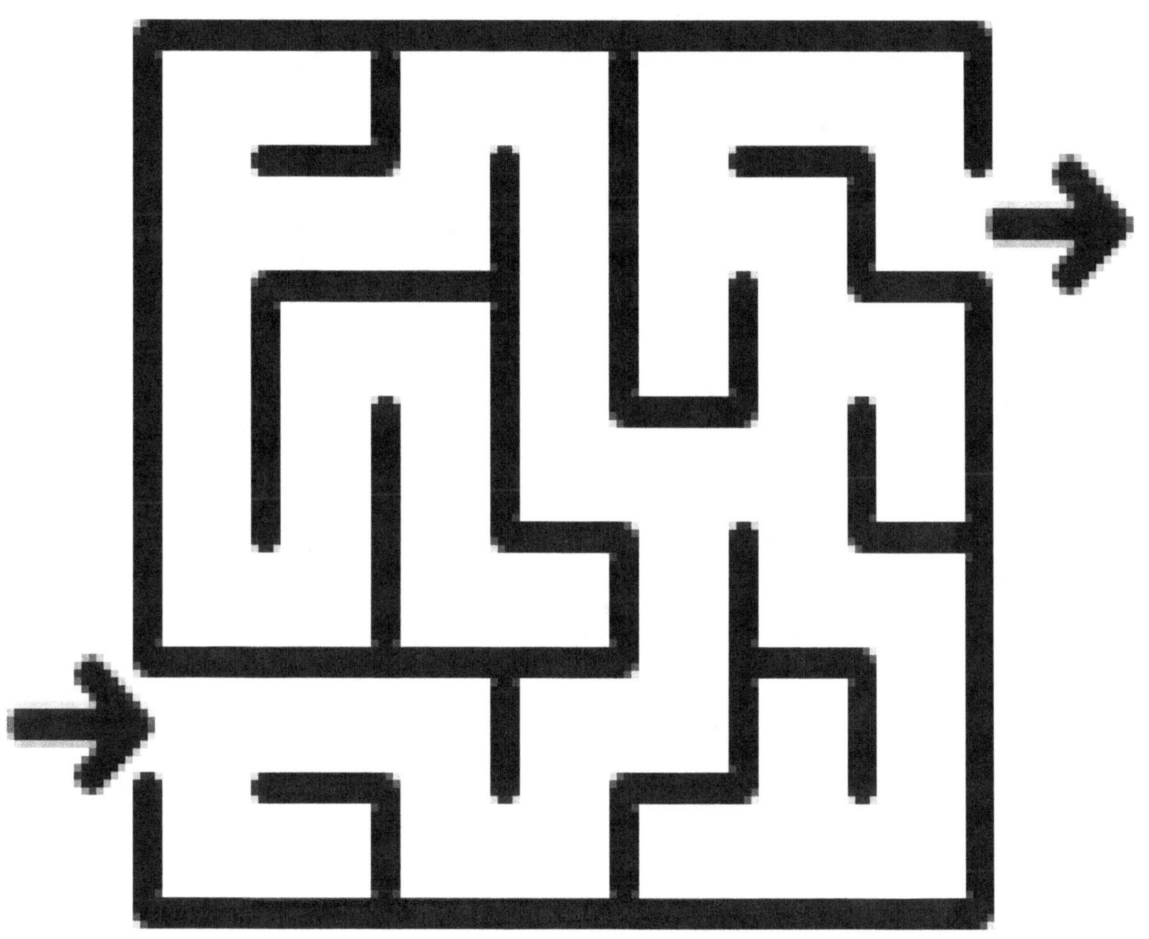

16
EASY

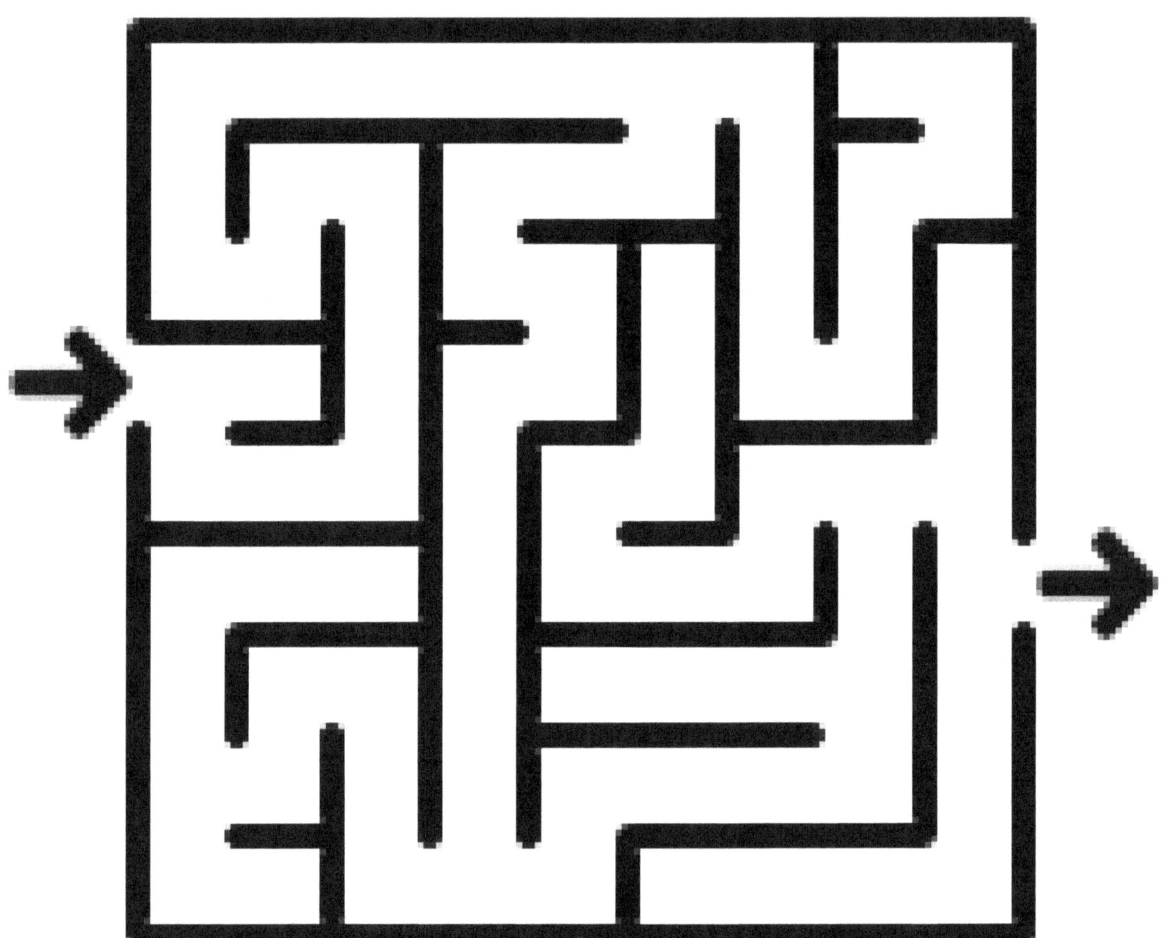

17
EASY

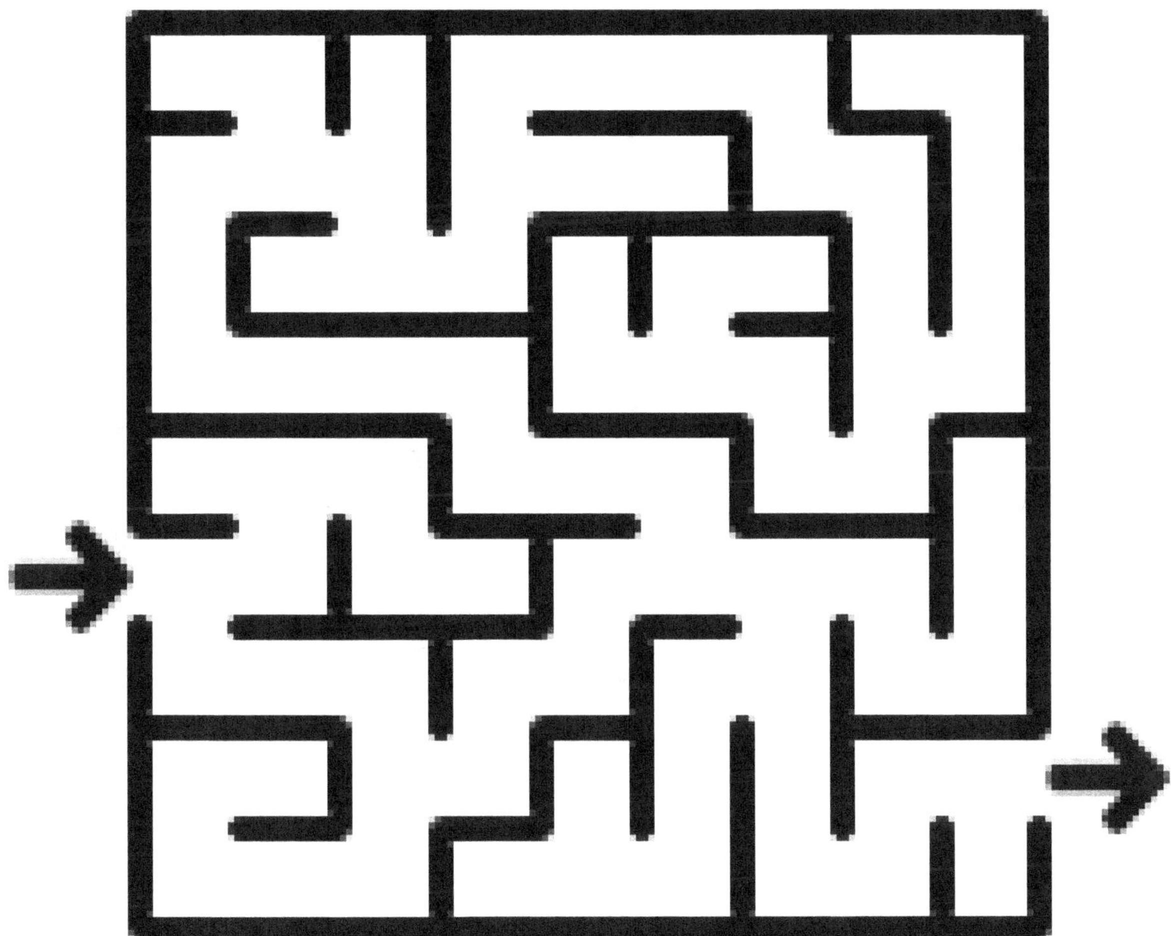

18
EASY

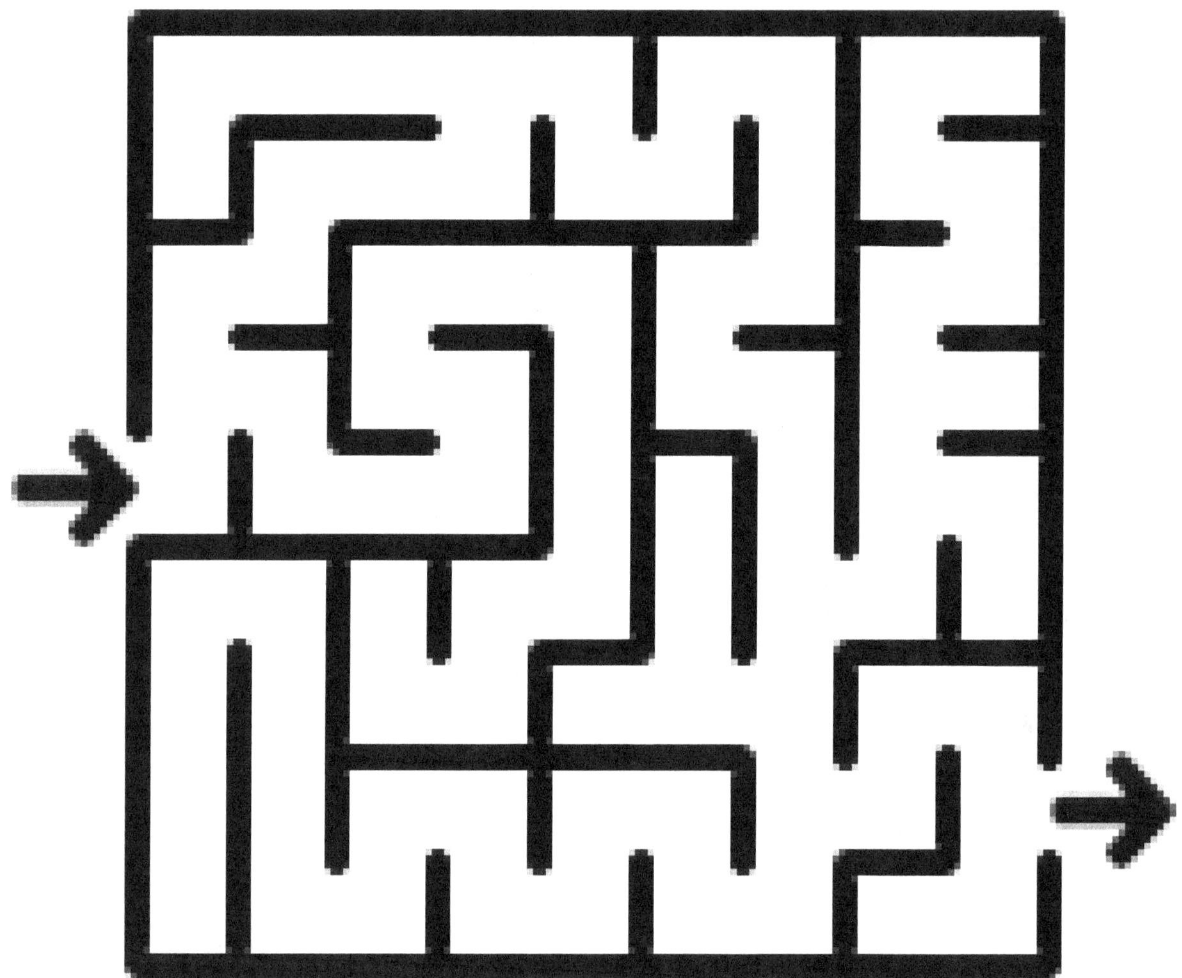

19
EASY

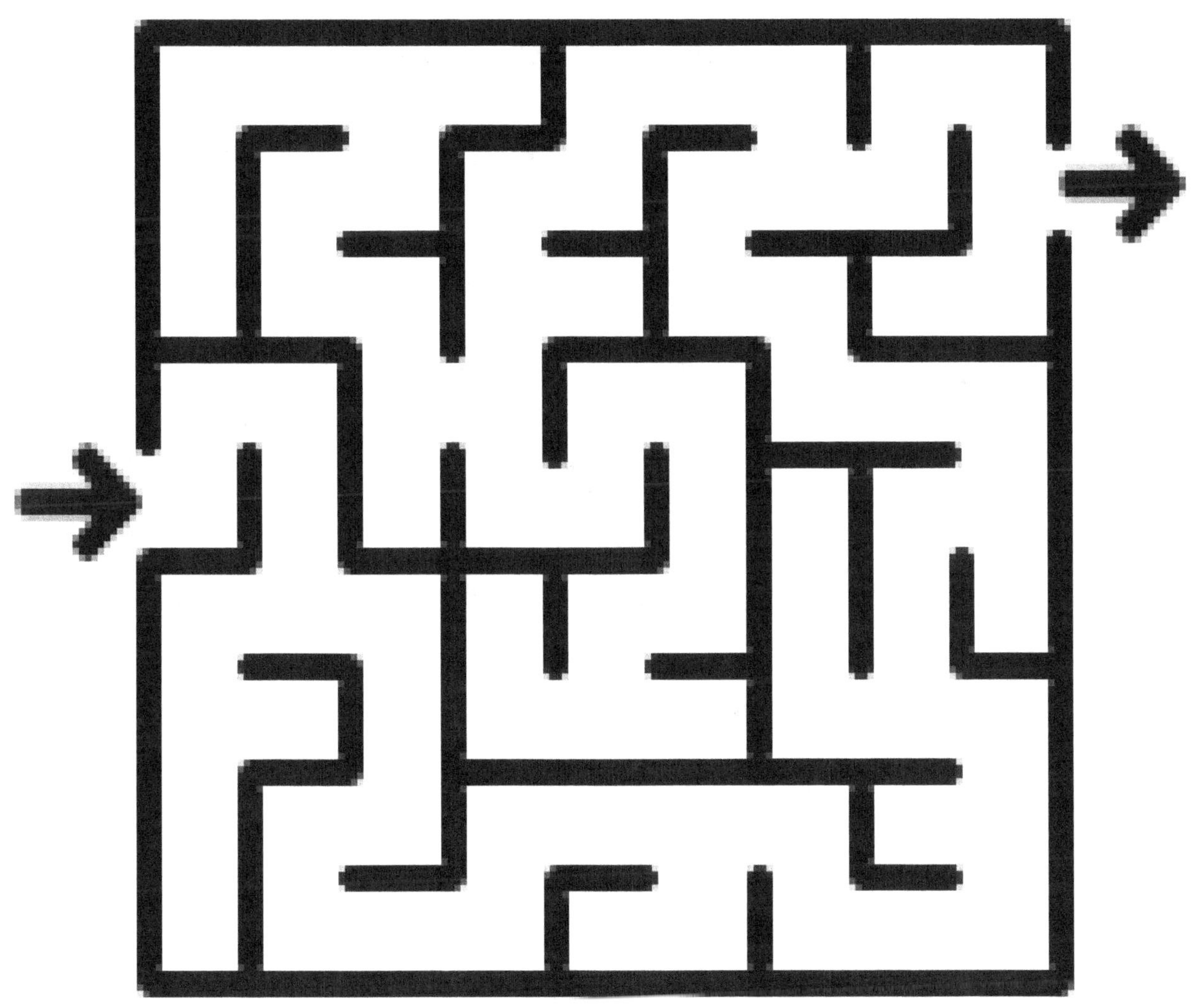

20
EASY

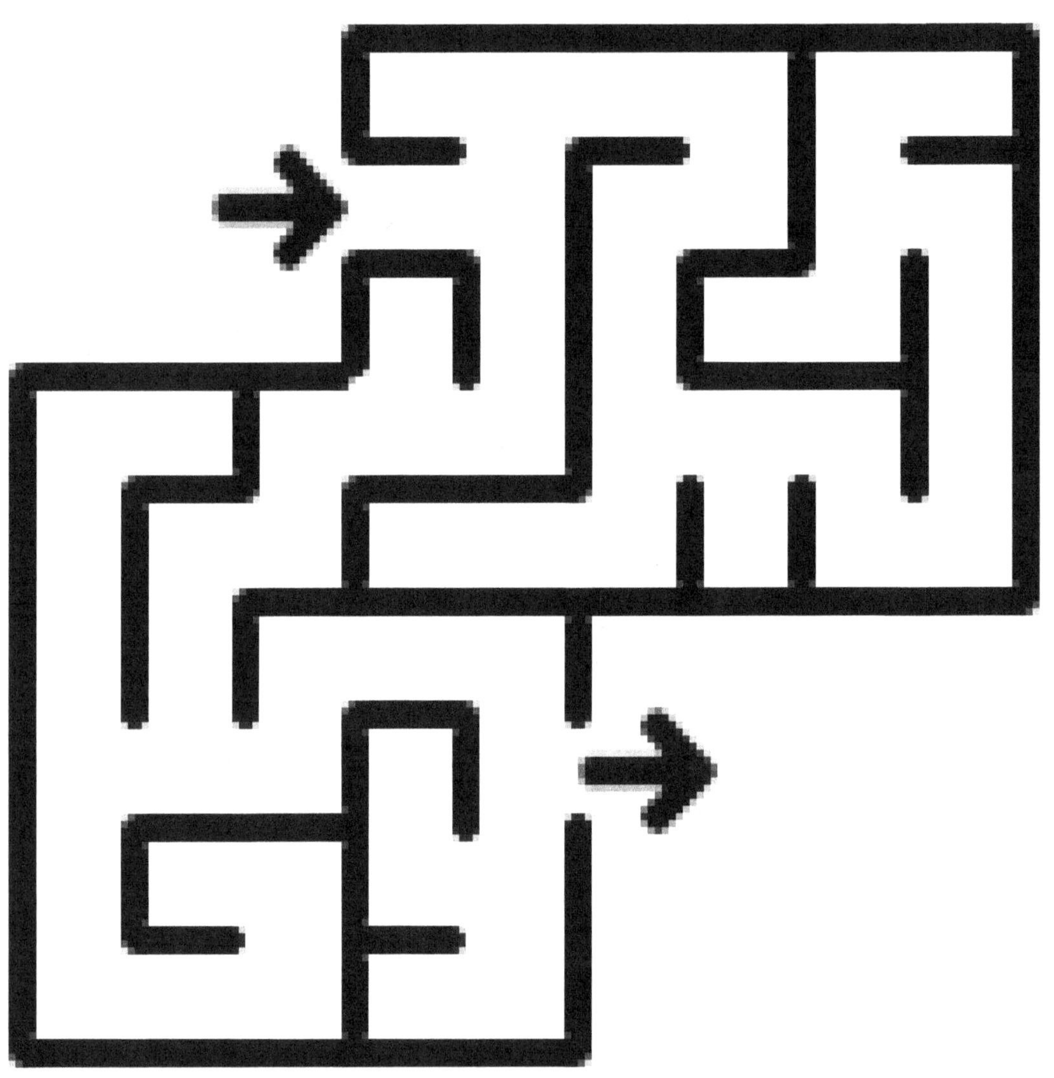

21
EASY

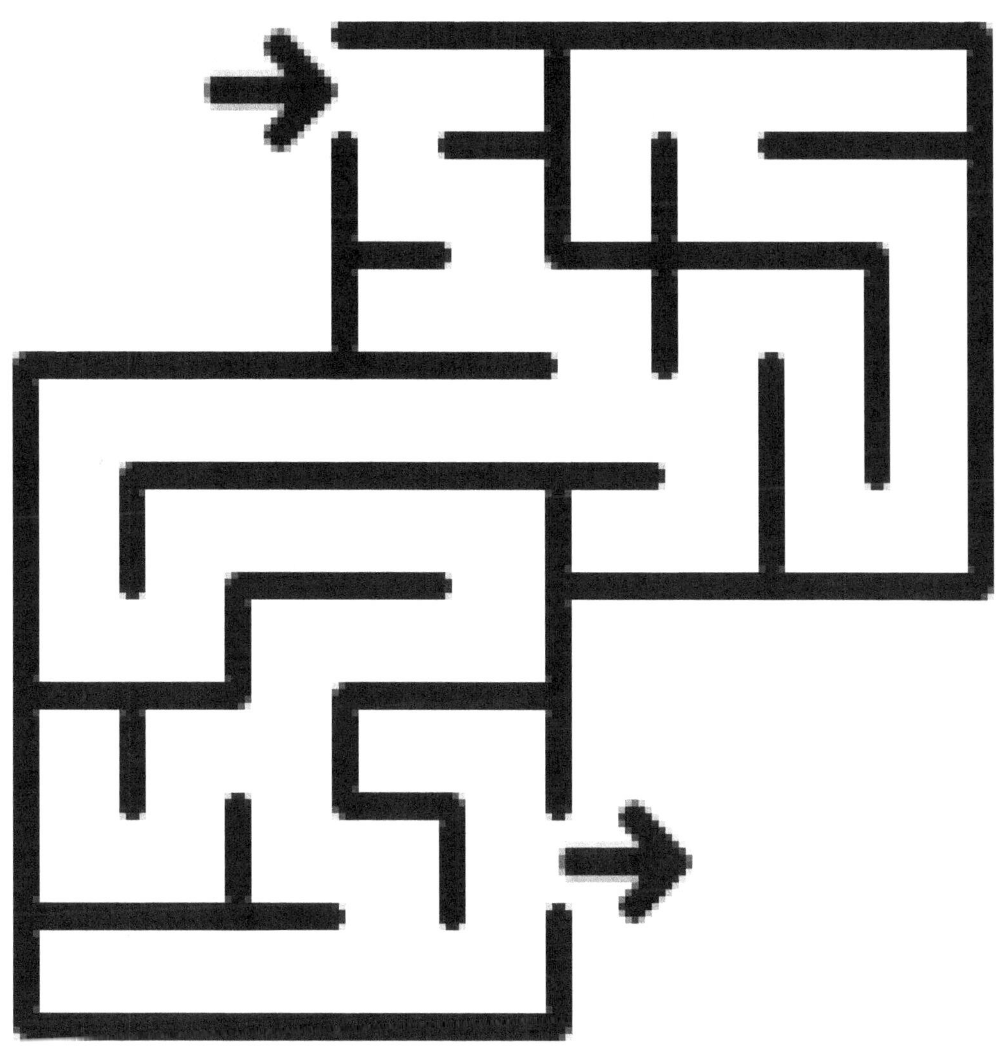

22
EASY

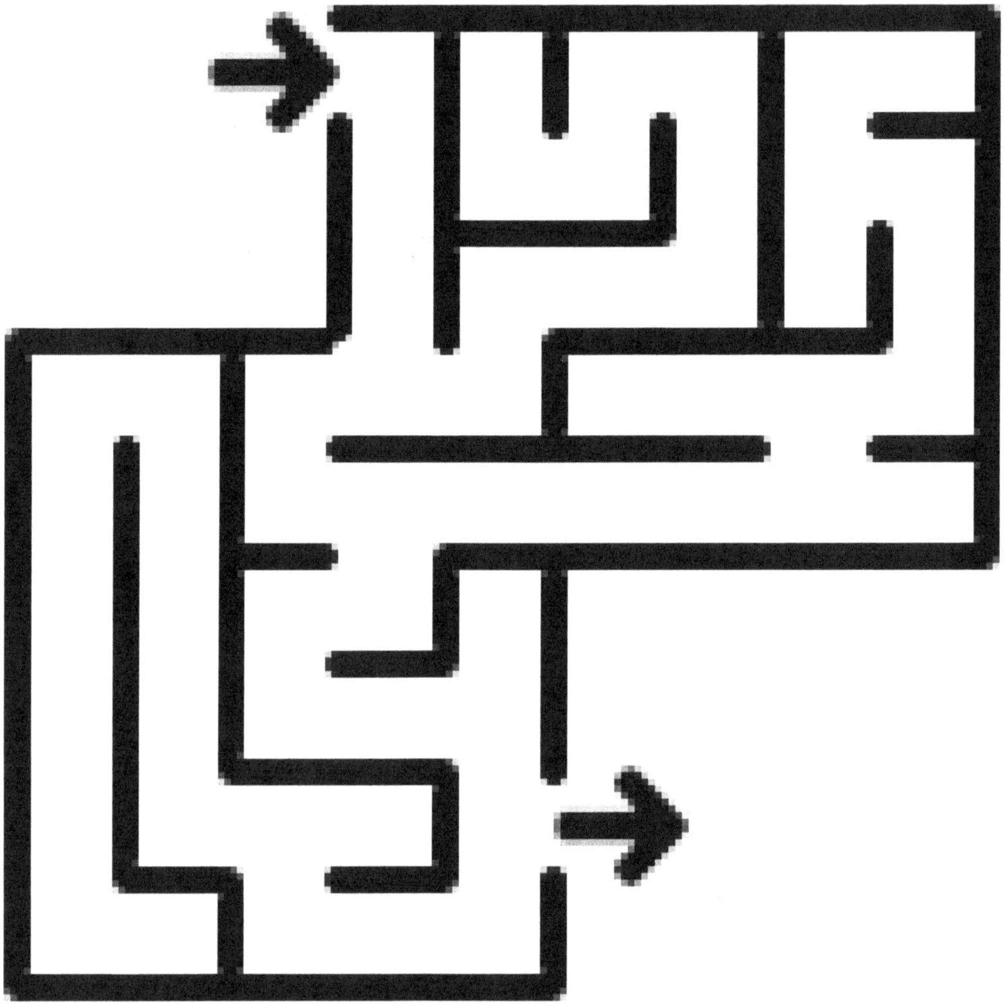

23
EASY

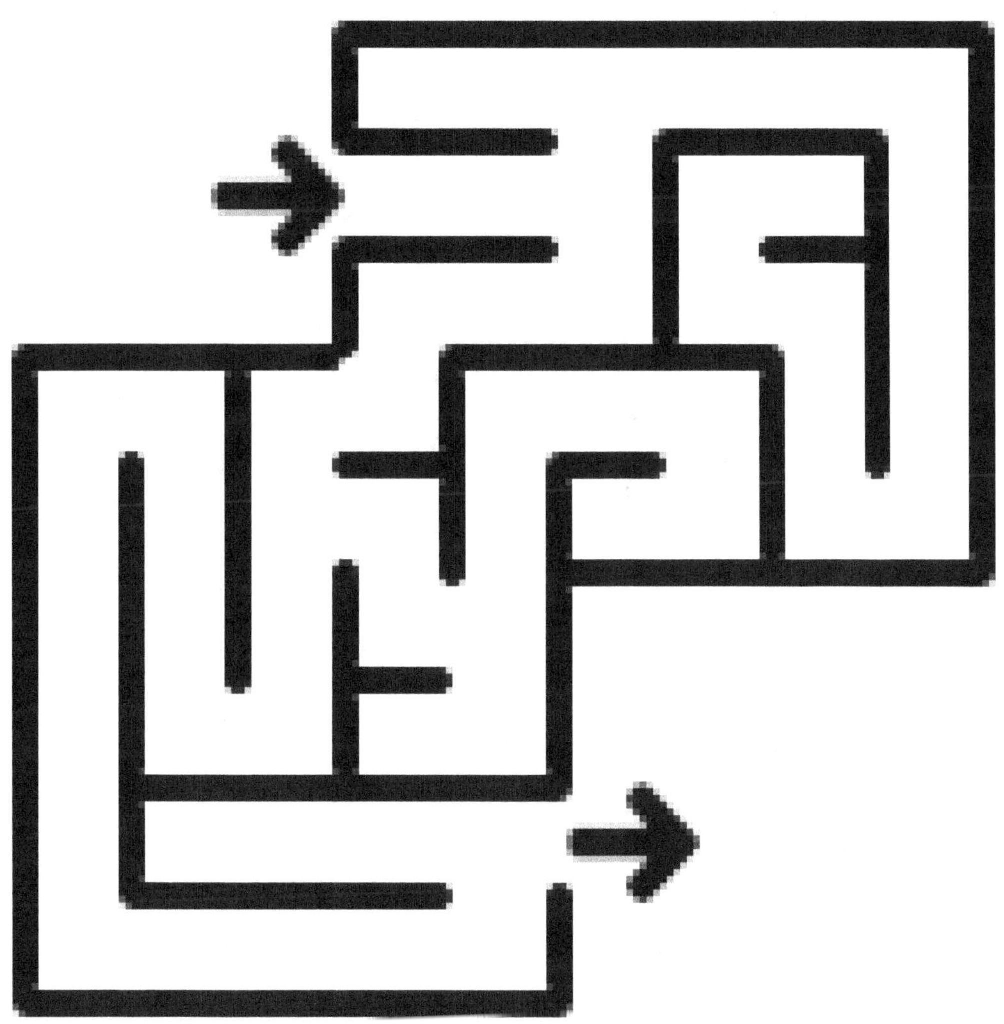

24
EASY

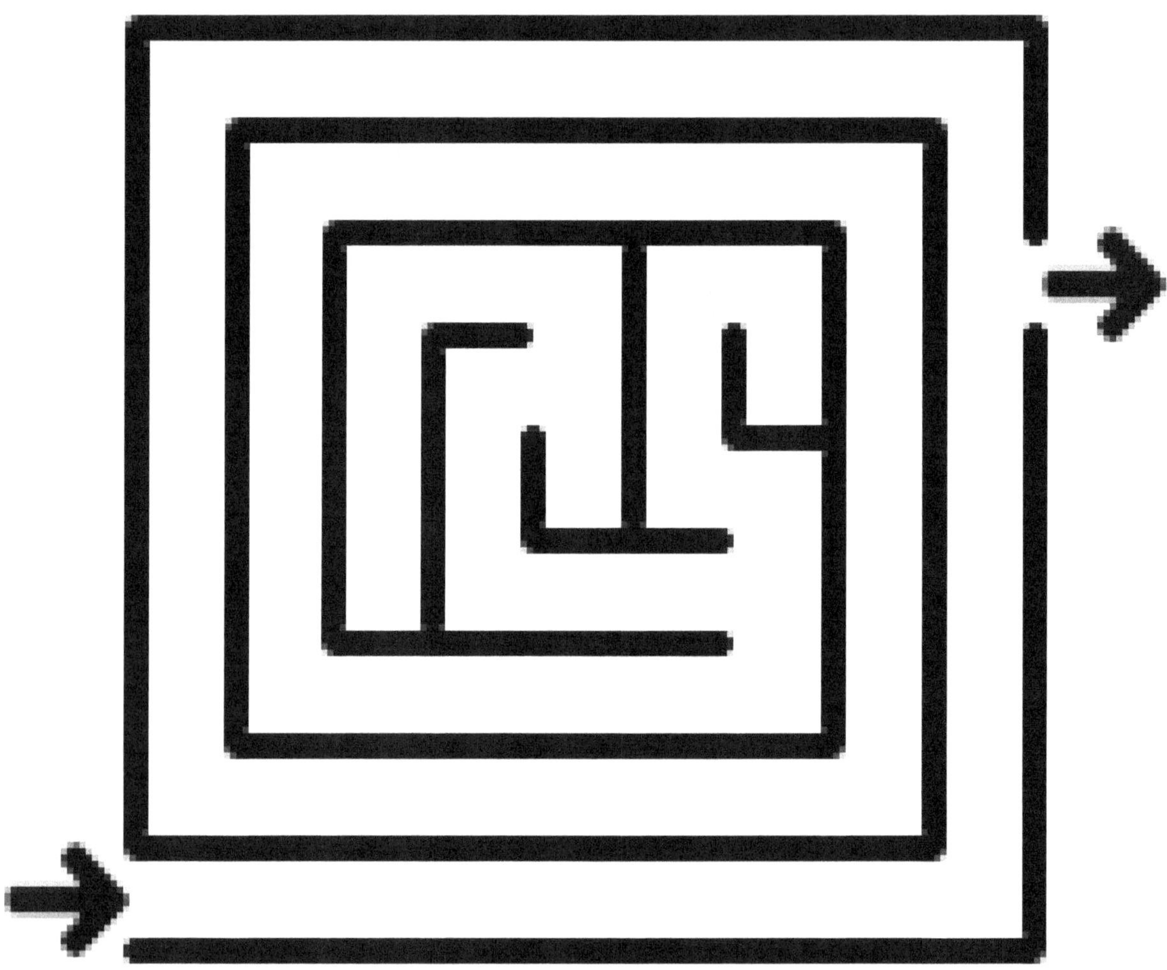

25
EASY

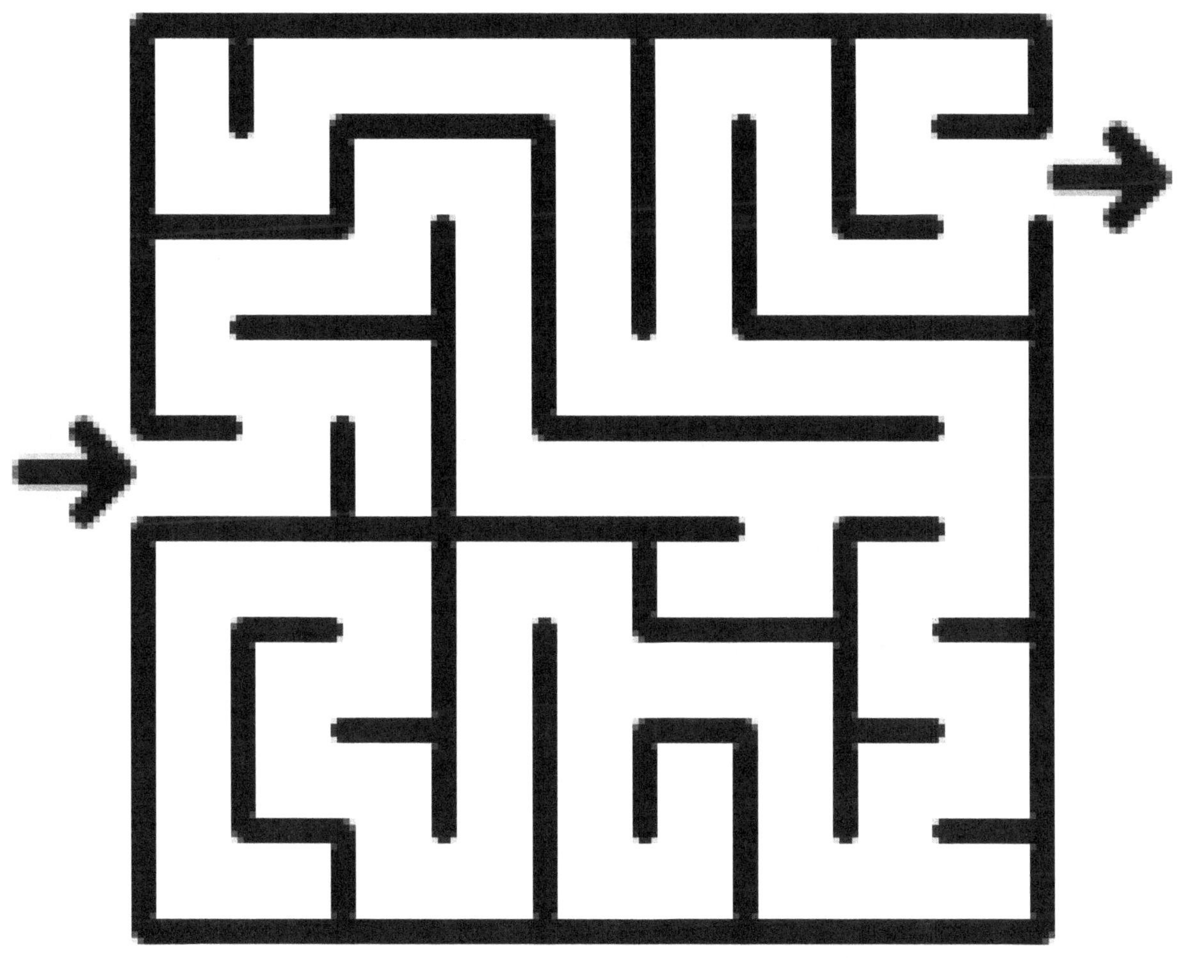

26
EASY

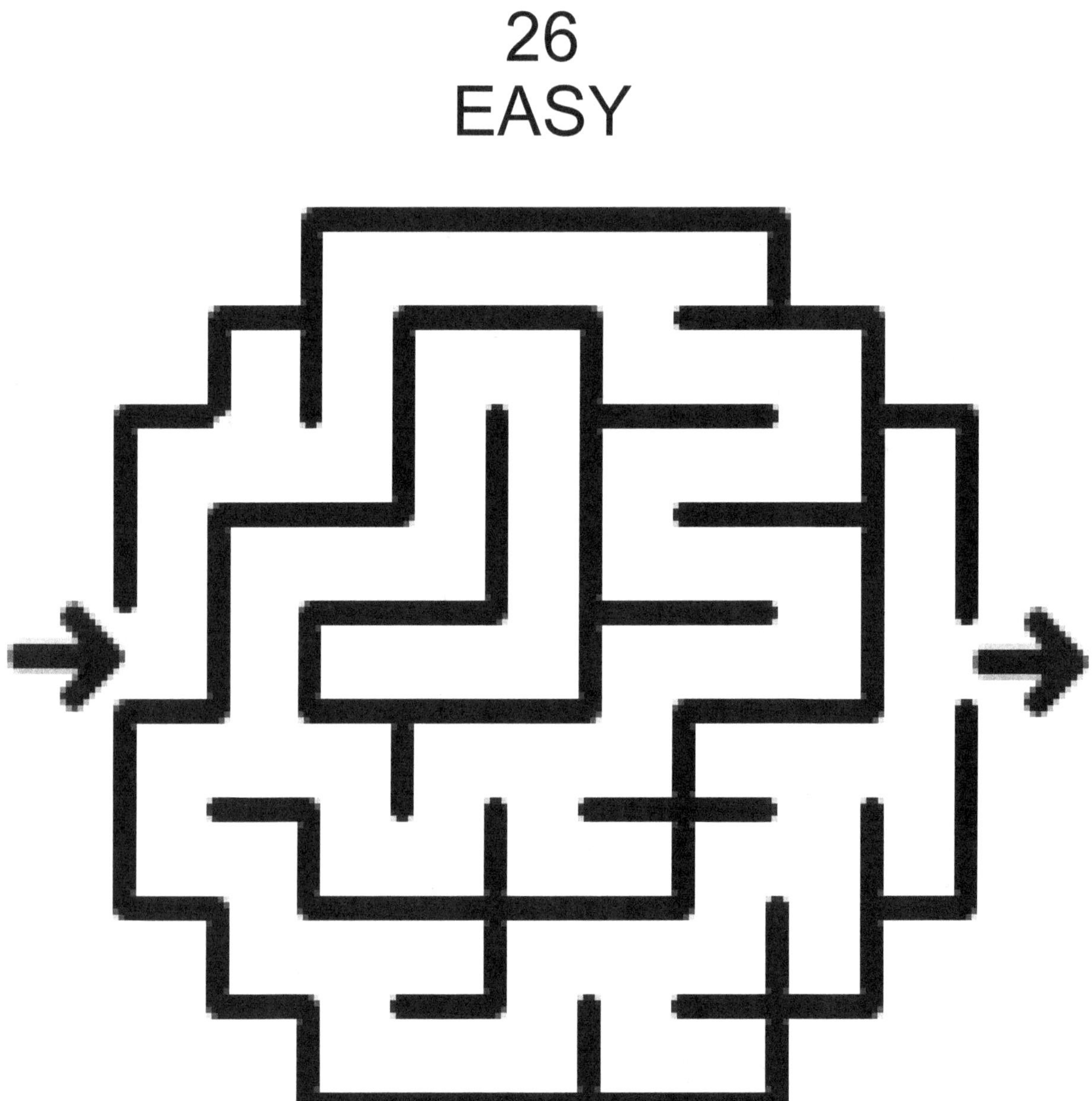

27
EASY

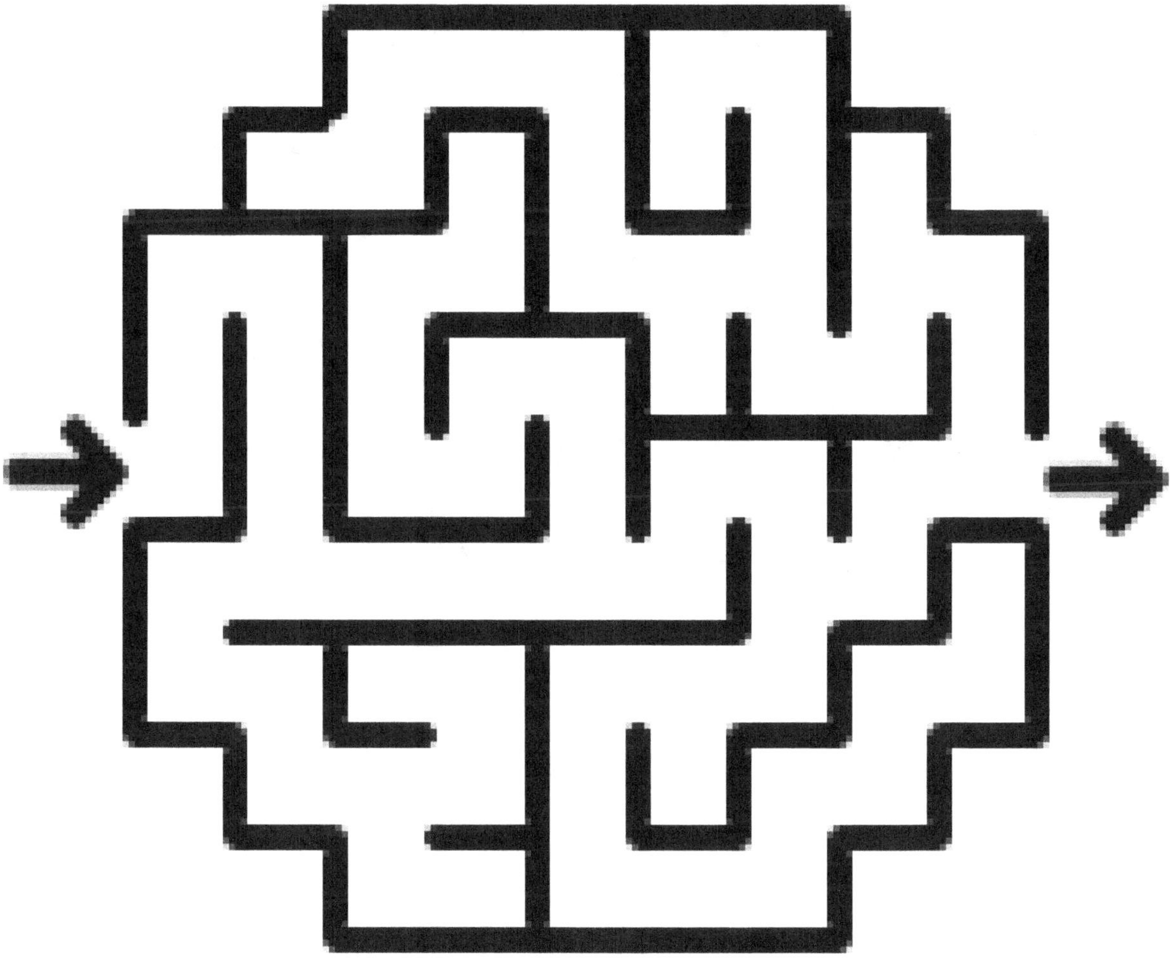

28
EASY

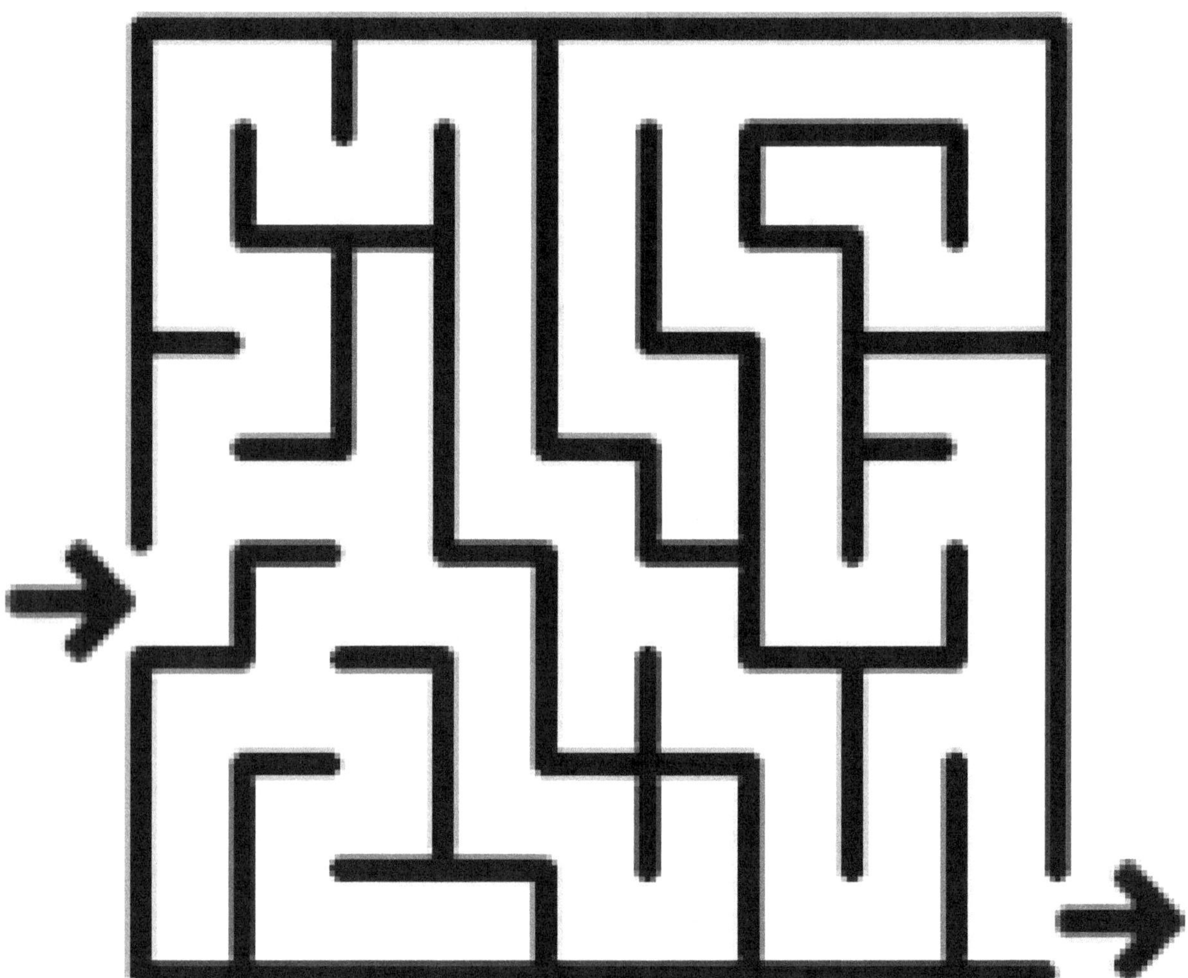

29
EASY

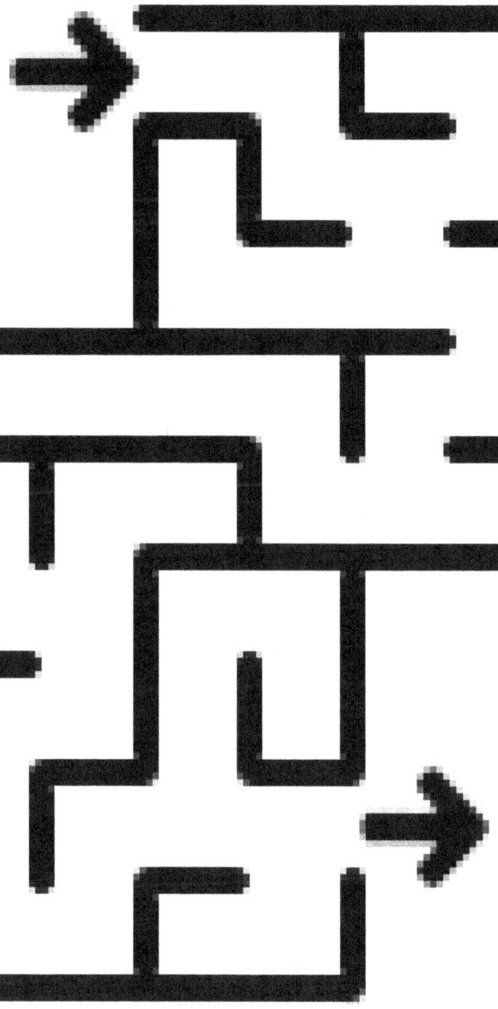

30
EASY

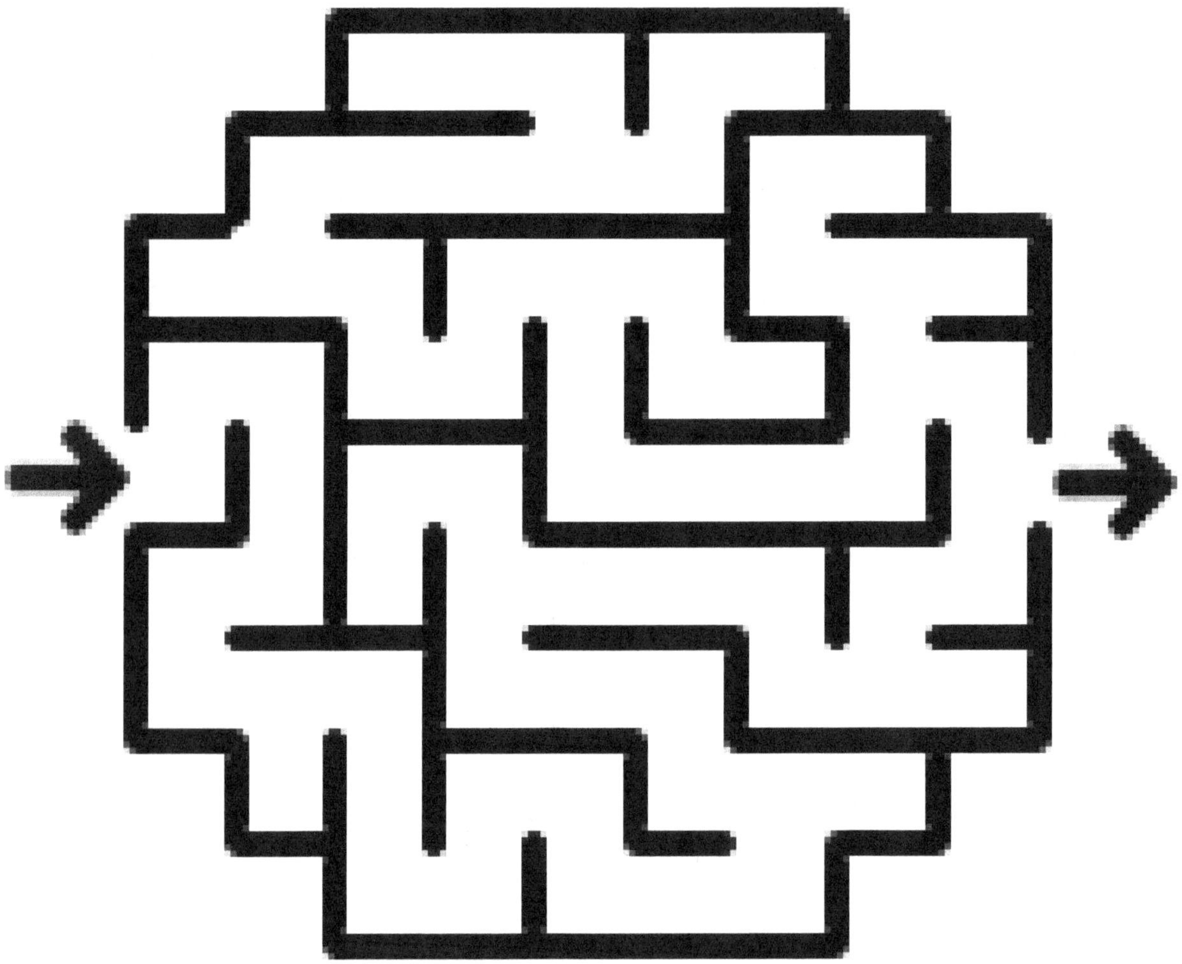

31
MEDIUM

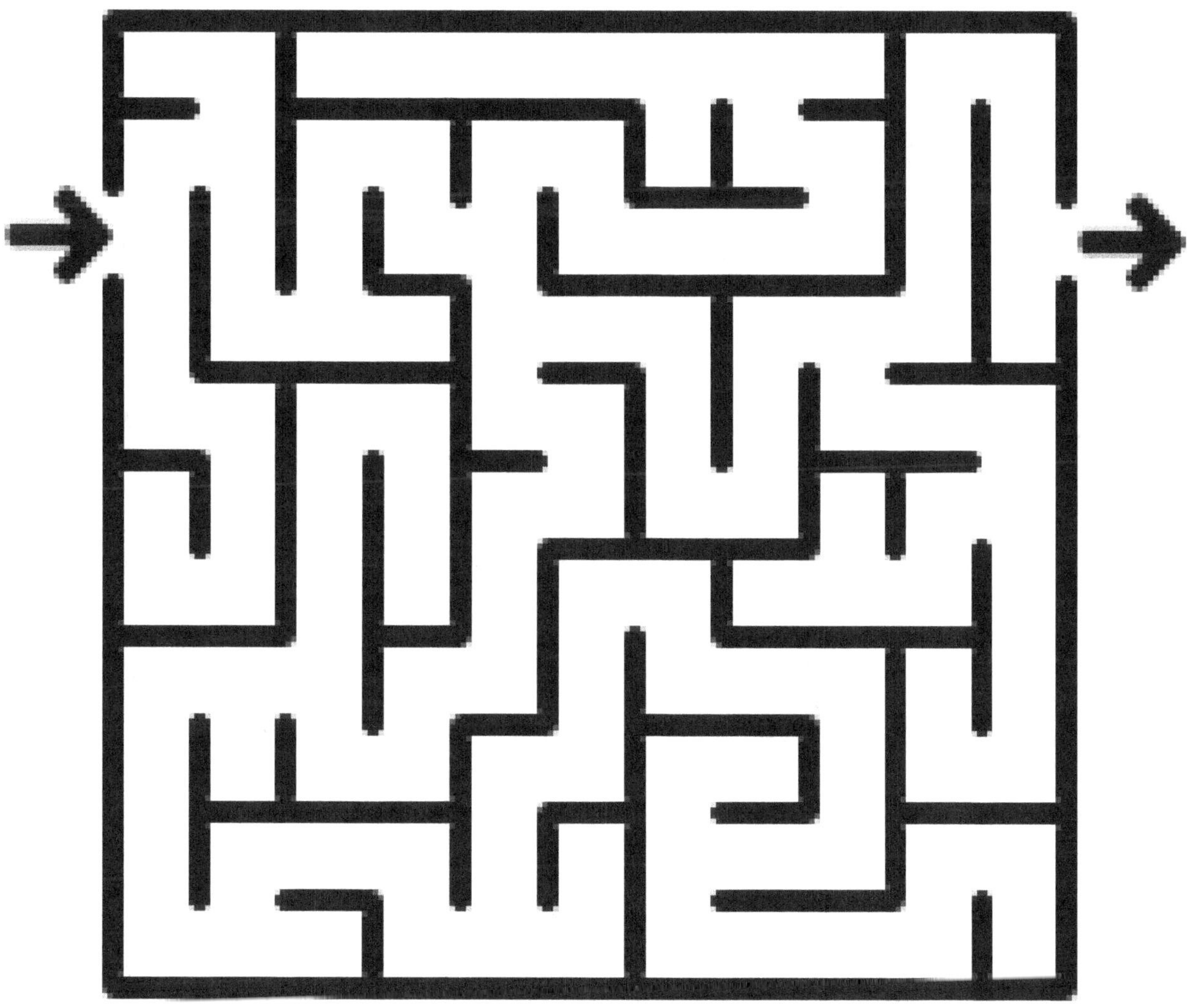

32
MEDIUM

33
MEDIUM

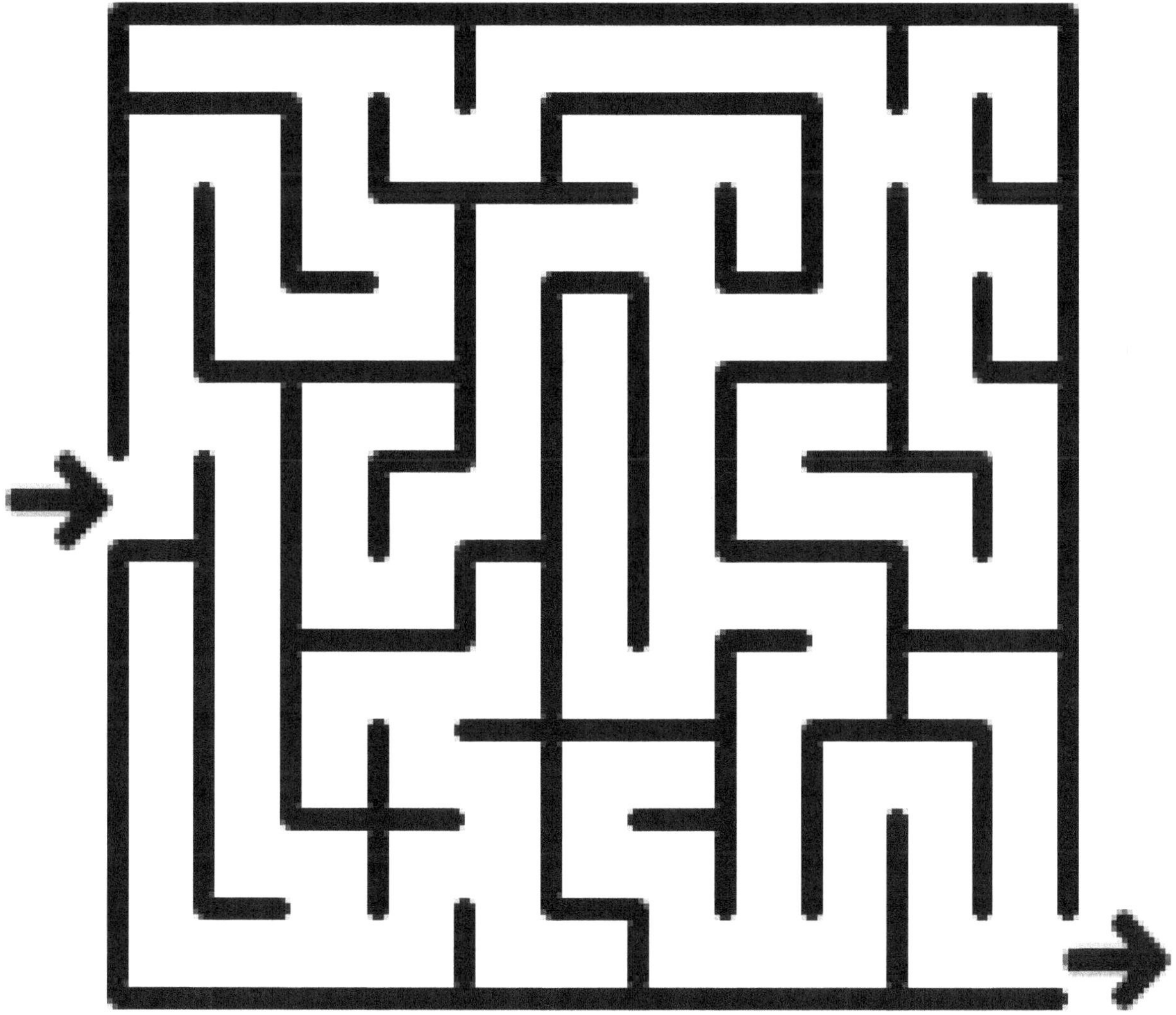

34
MEDIUM

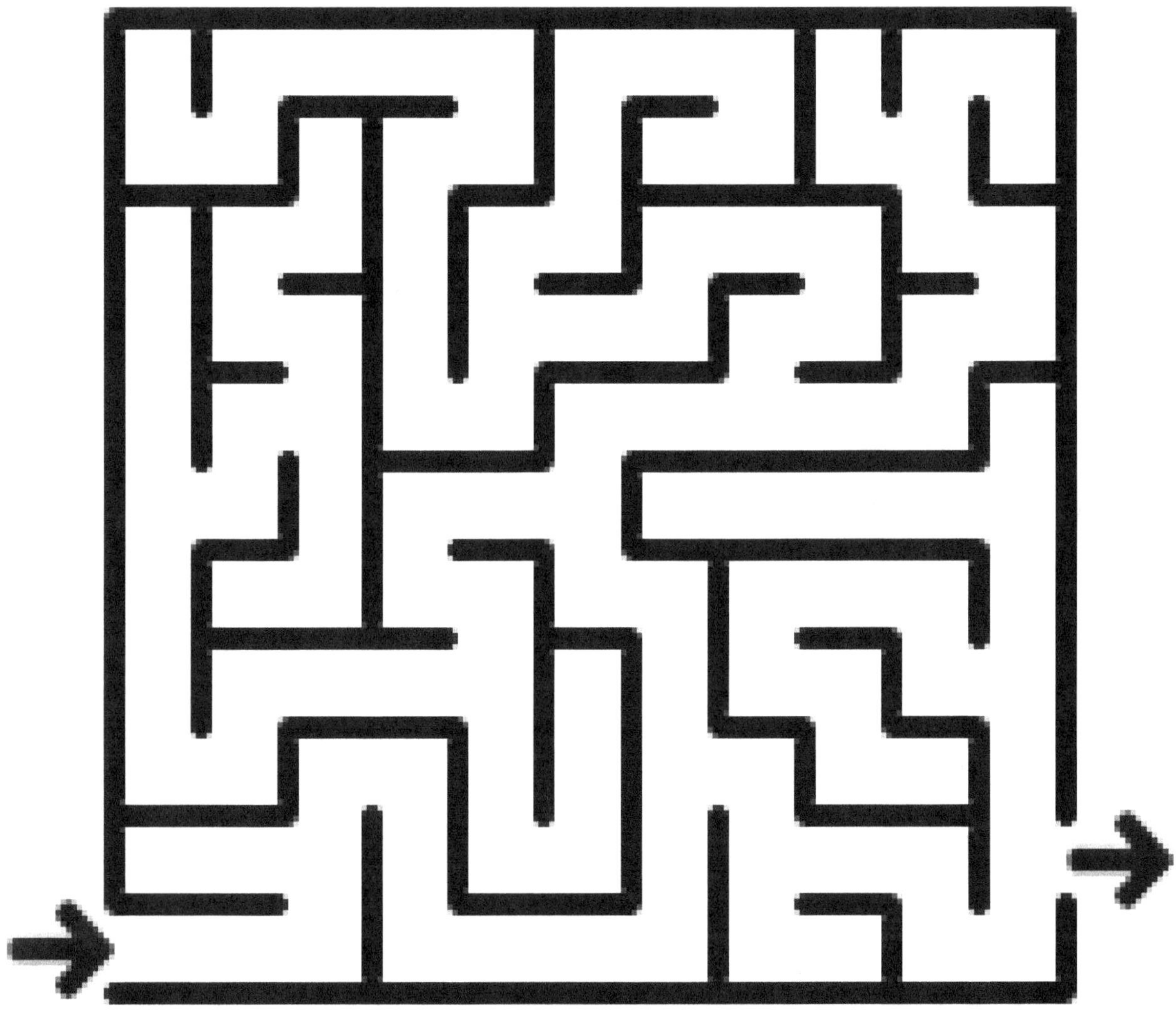

35
MEDIUM

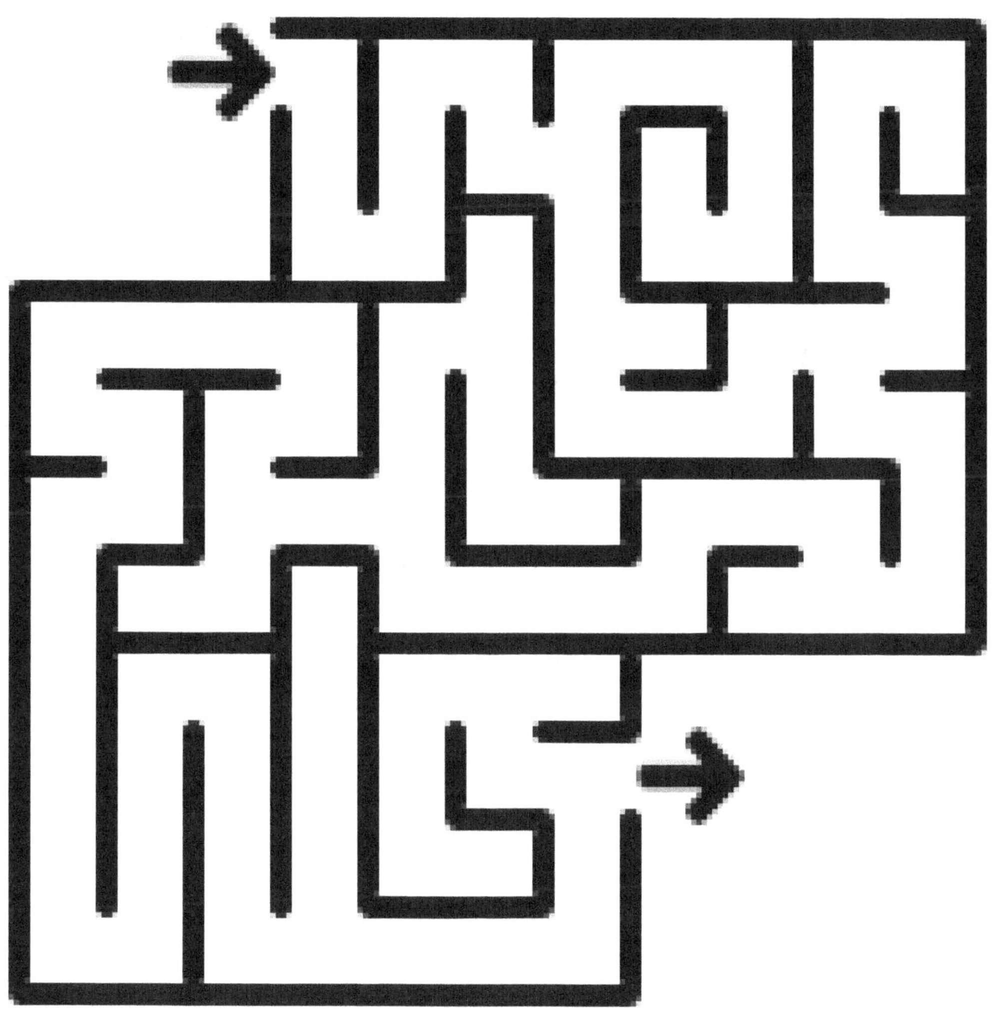

36
MEDIUM

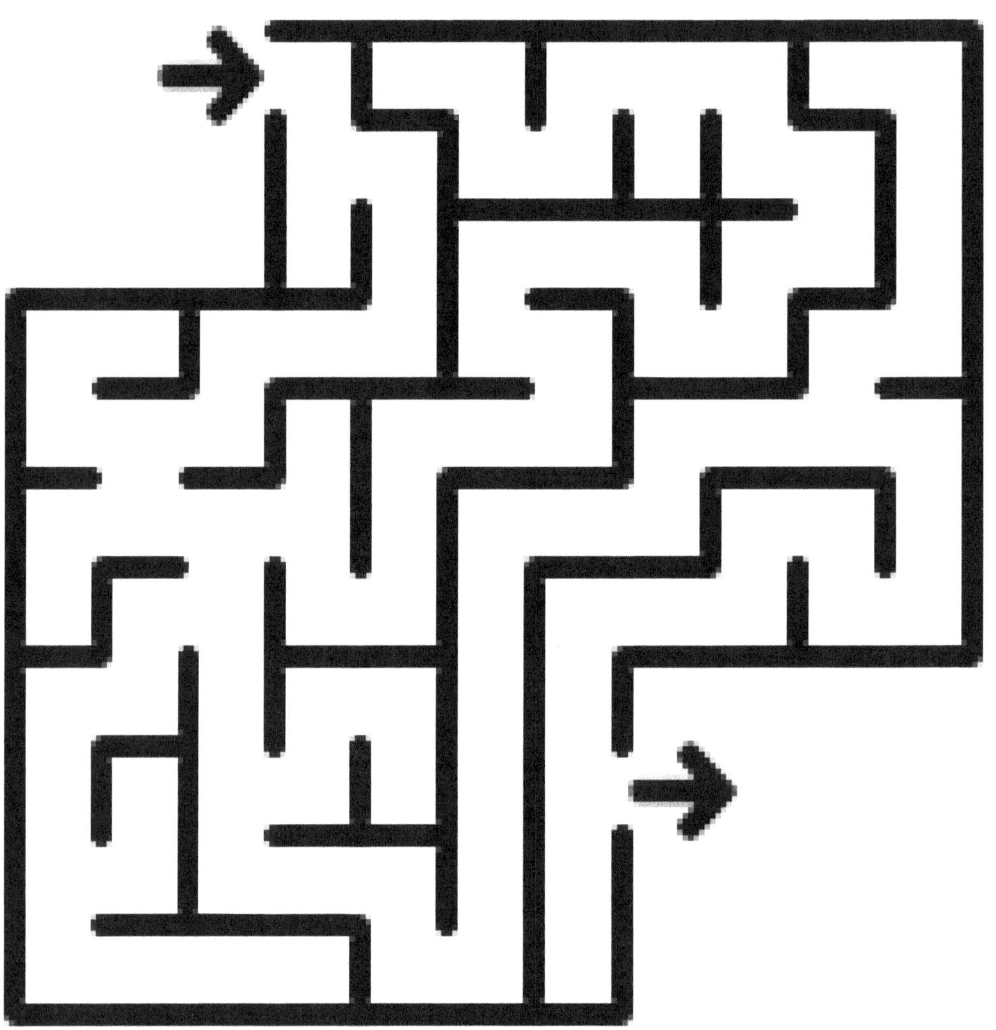

37
MEDIUM

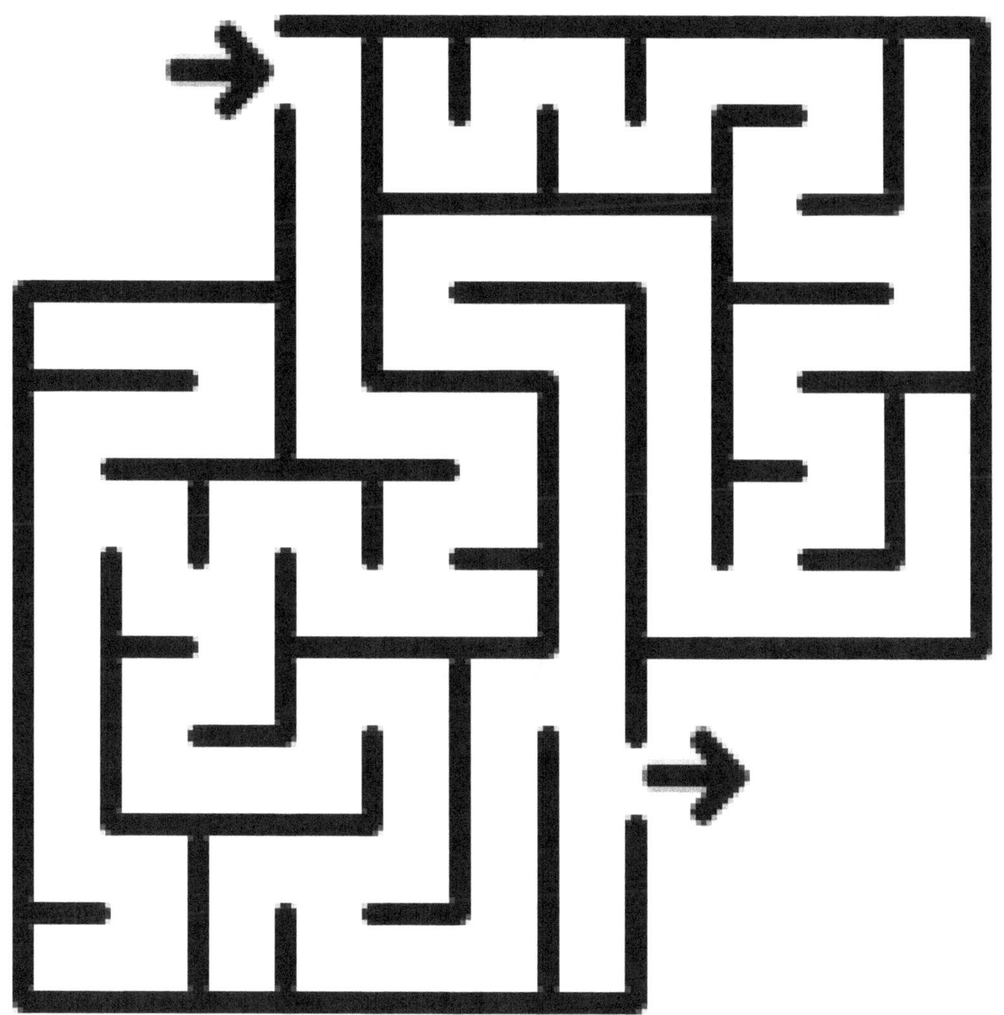

38
MEDIUM

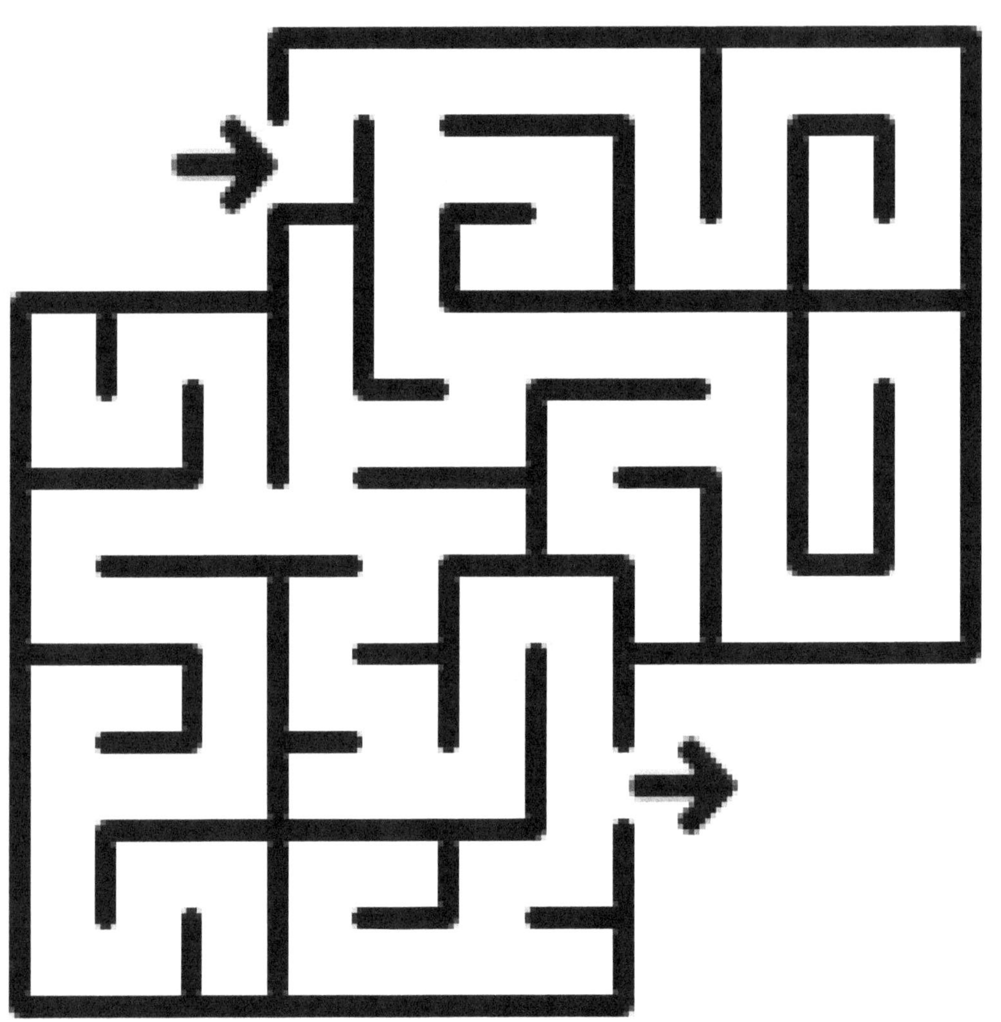

39
MEDIUM

40
MEDIUM

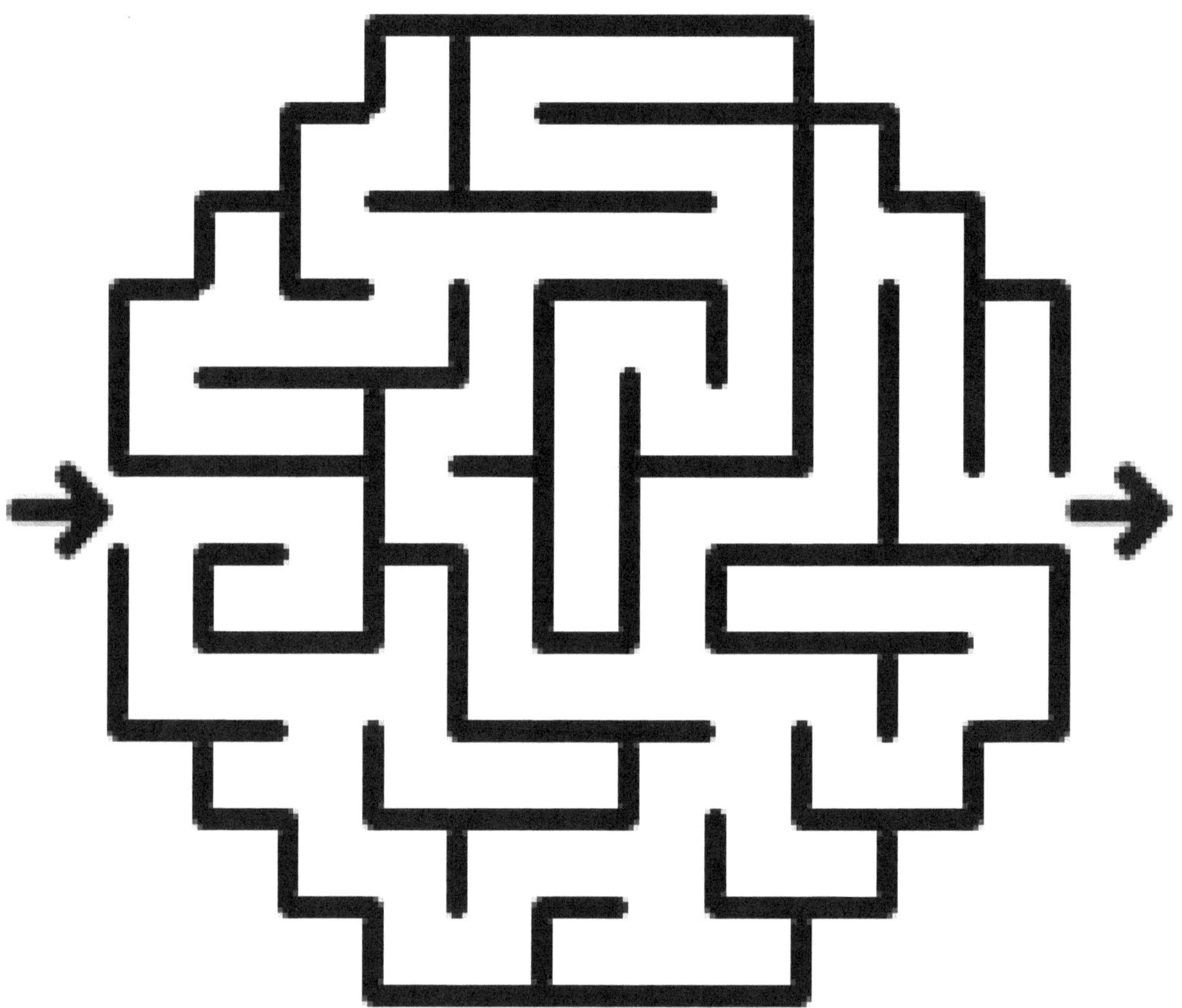

41
MEDIUM

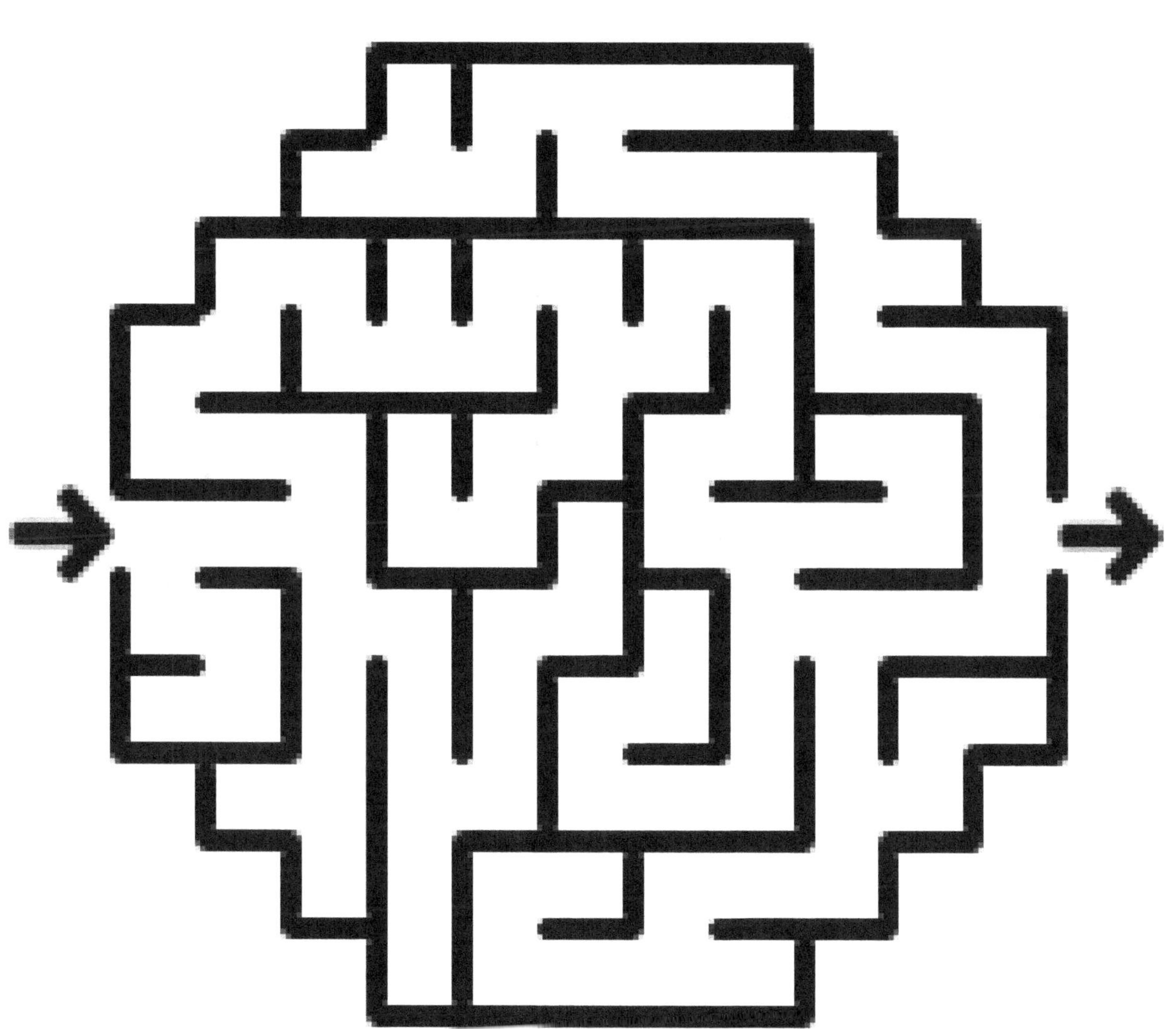

42
MEDIUM

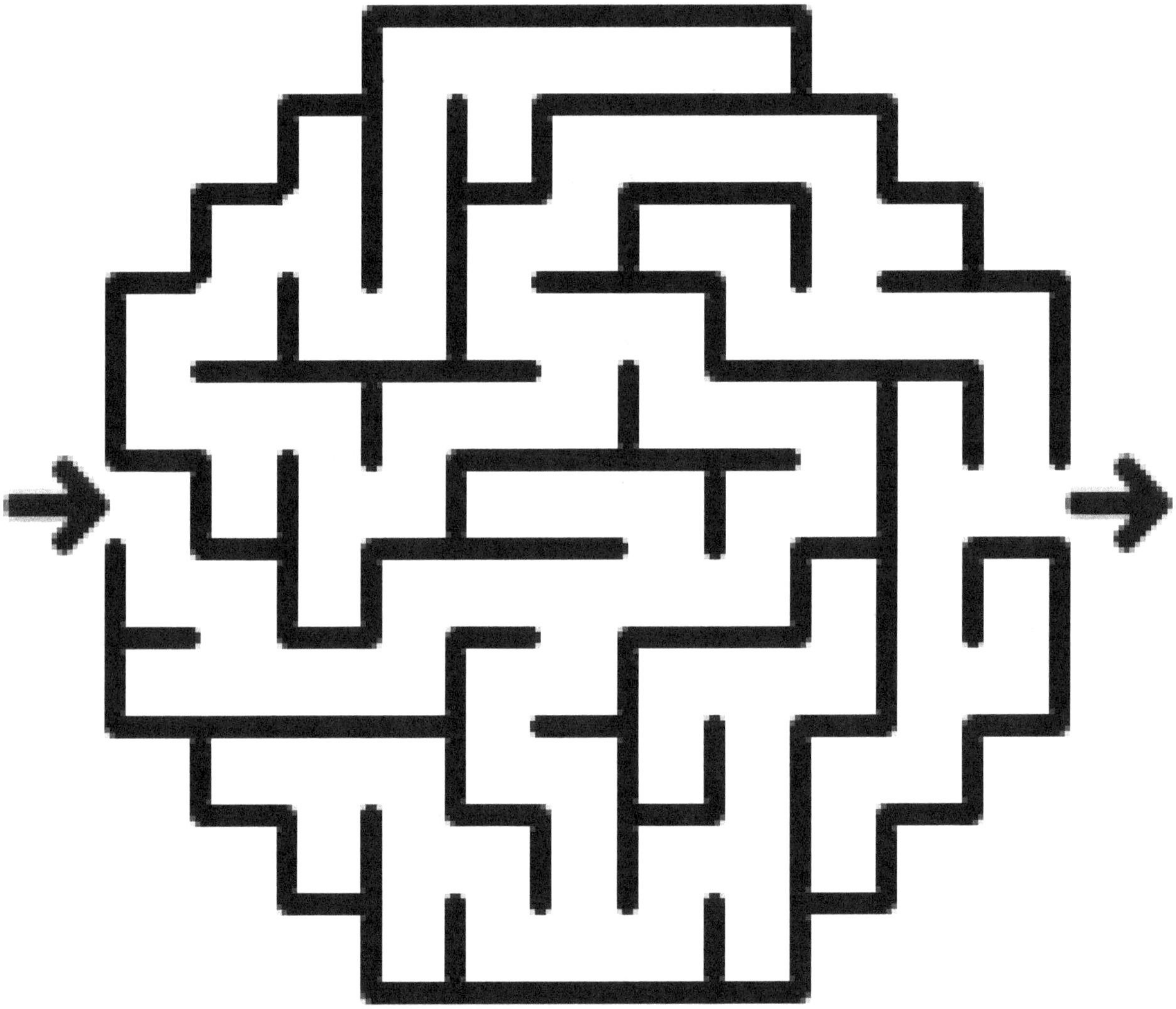

43
MEDIUM

44
MEDIUM

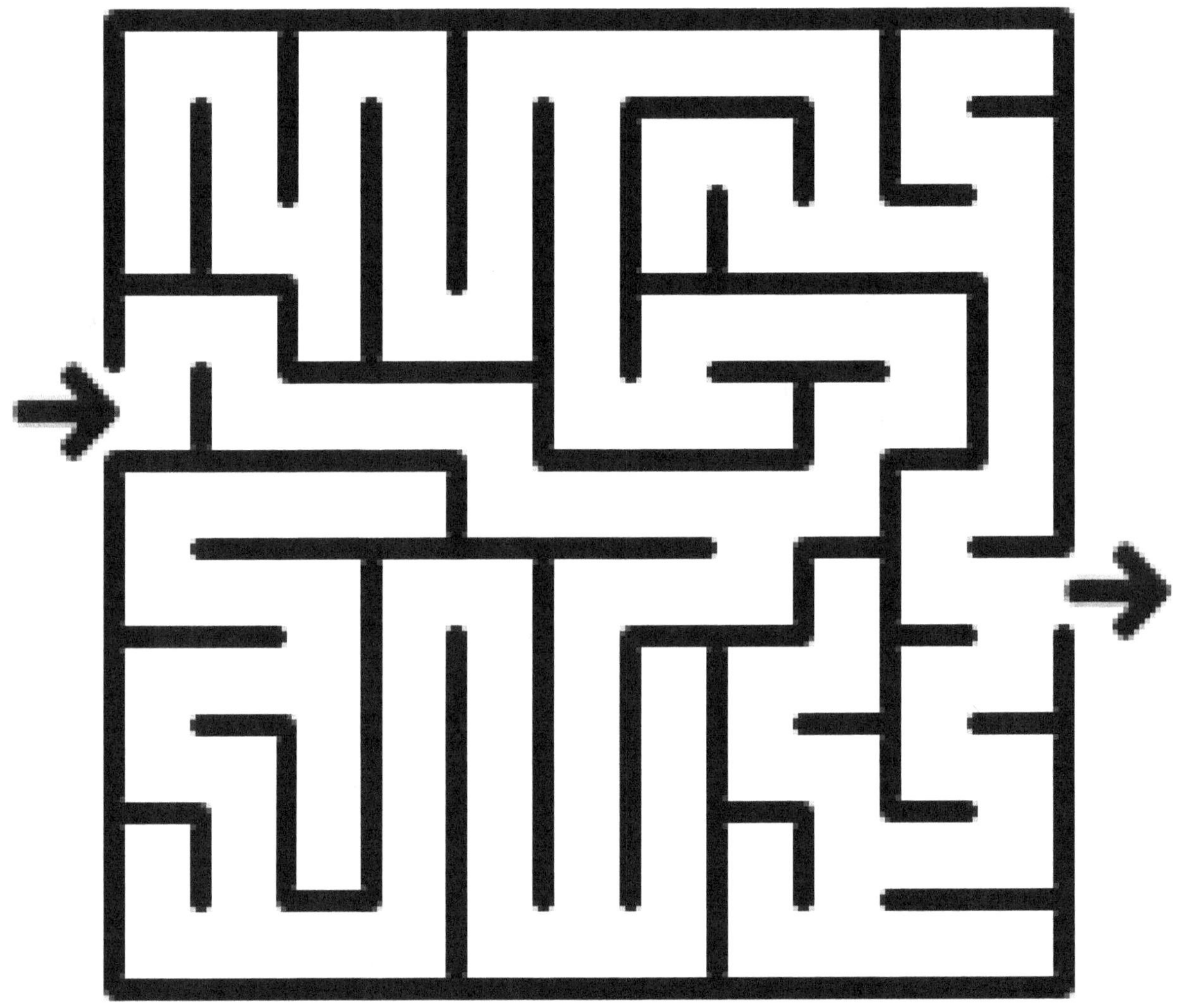

45
MEDIUM

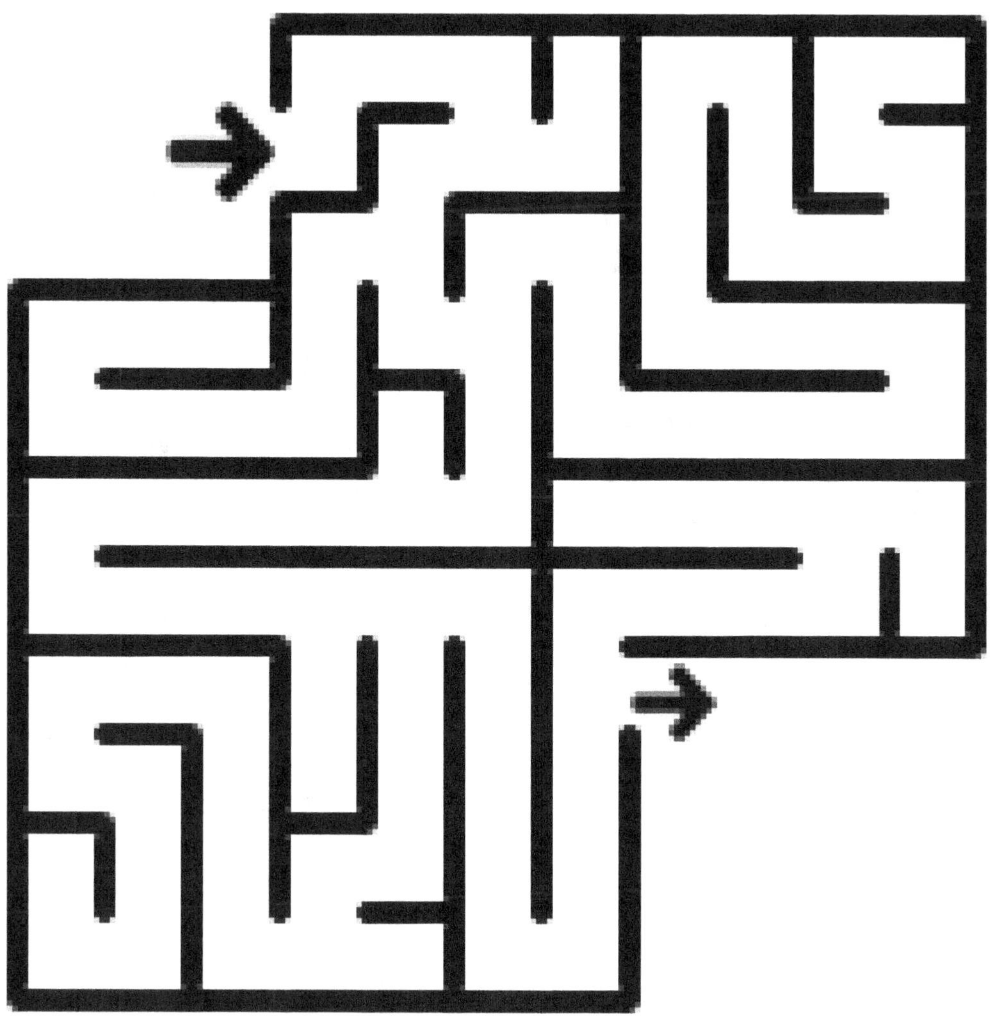

46
DIFFICULT

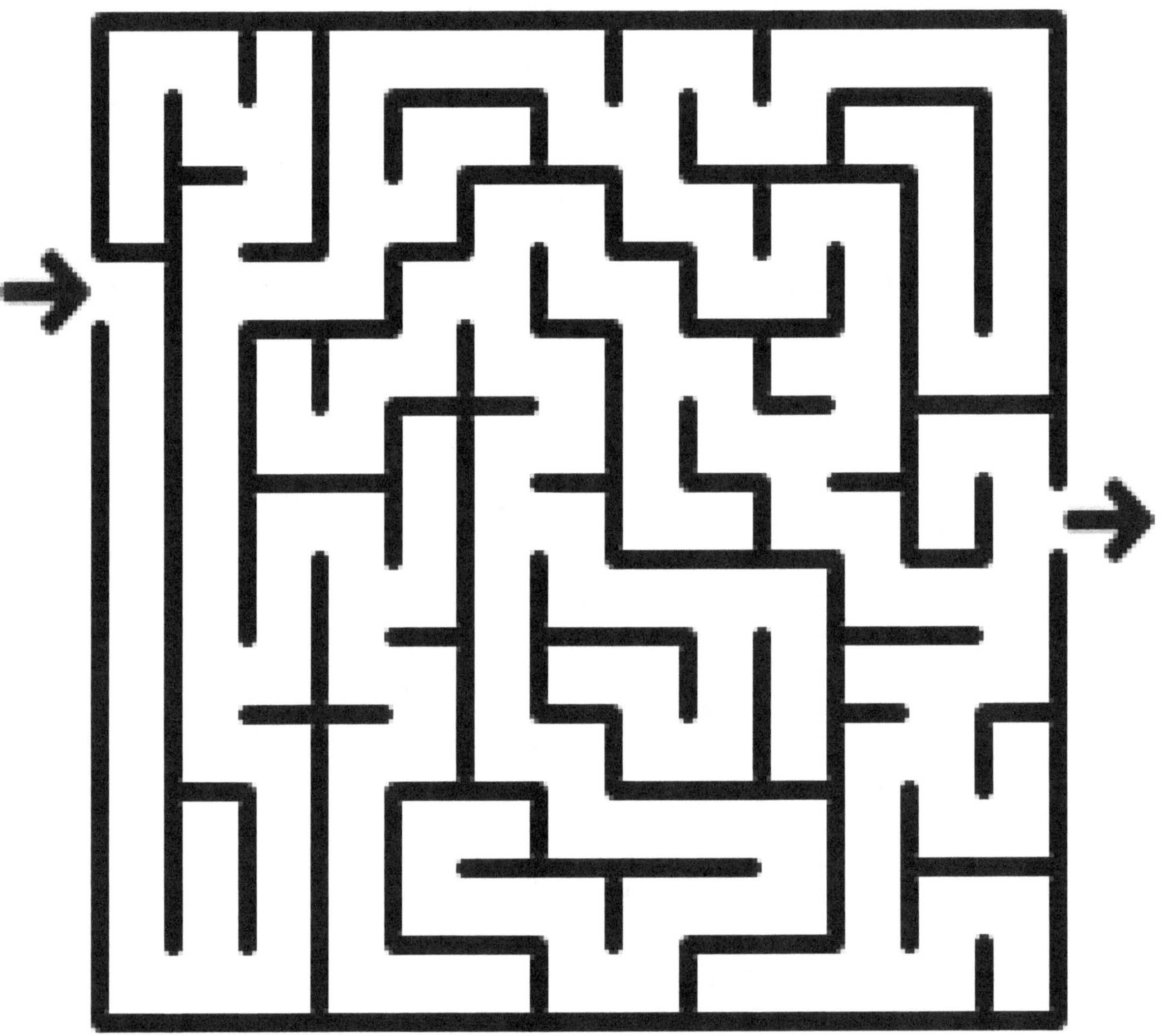

47
DIFFICULT

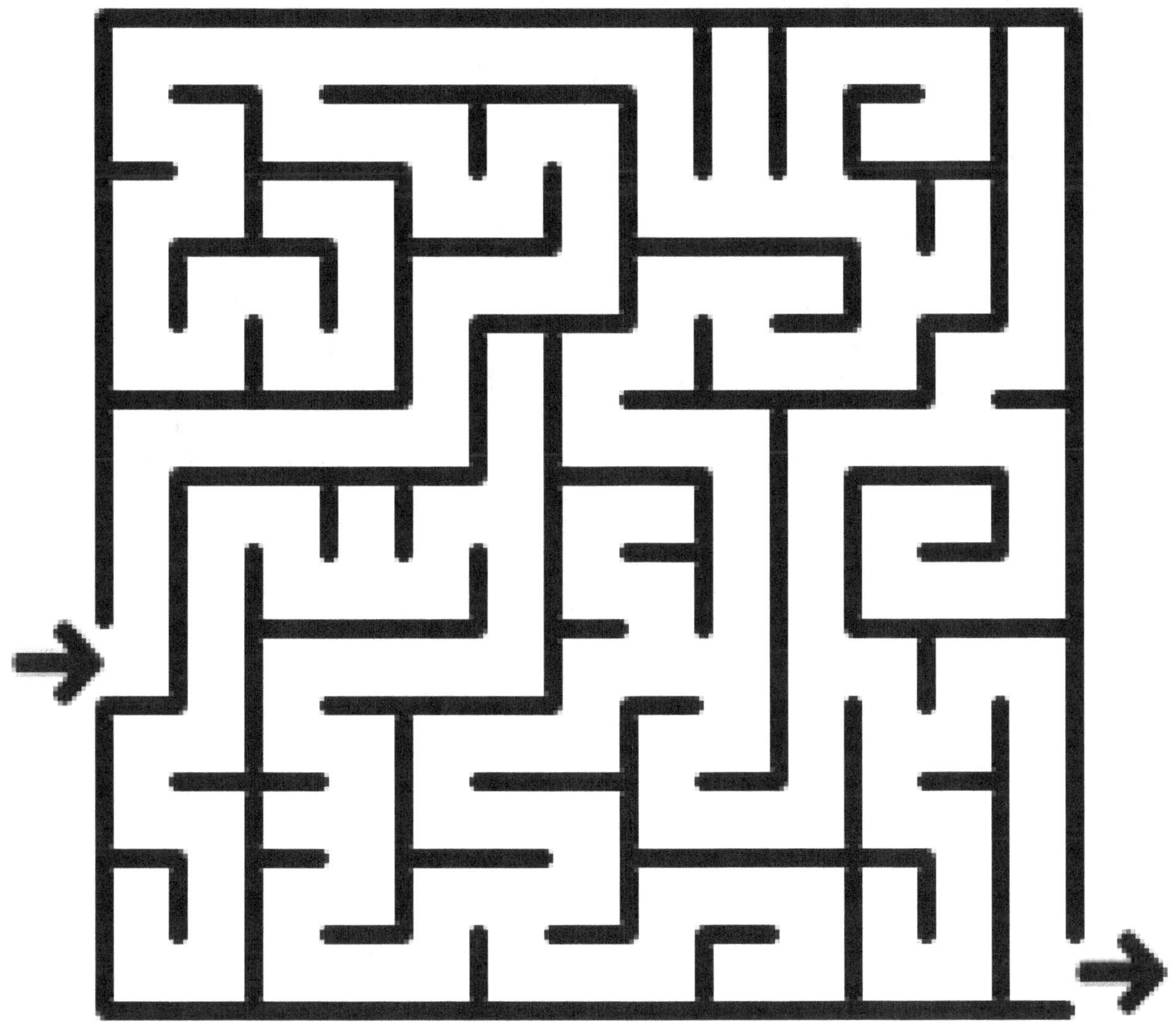

48
DIFFICULT

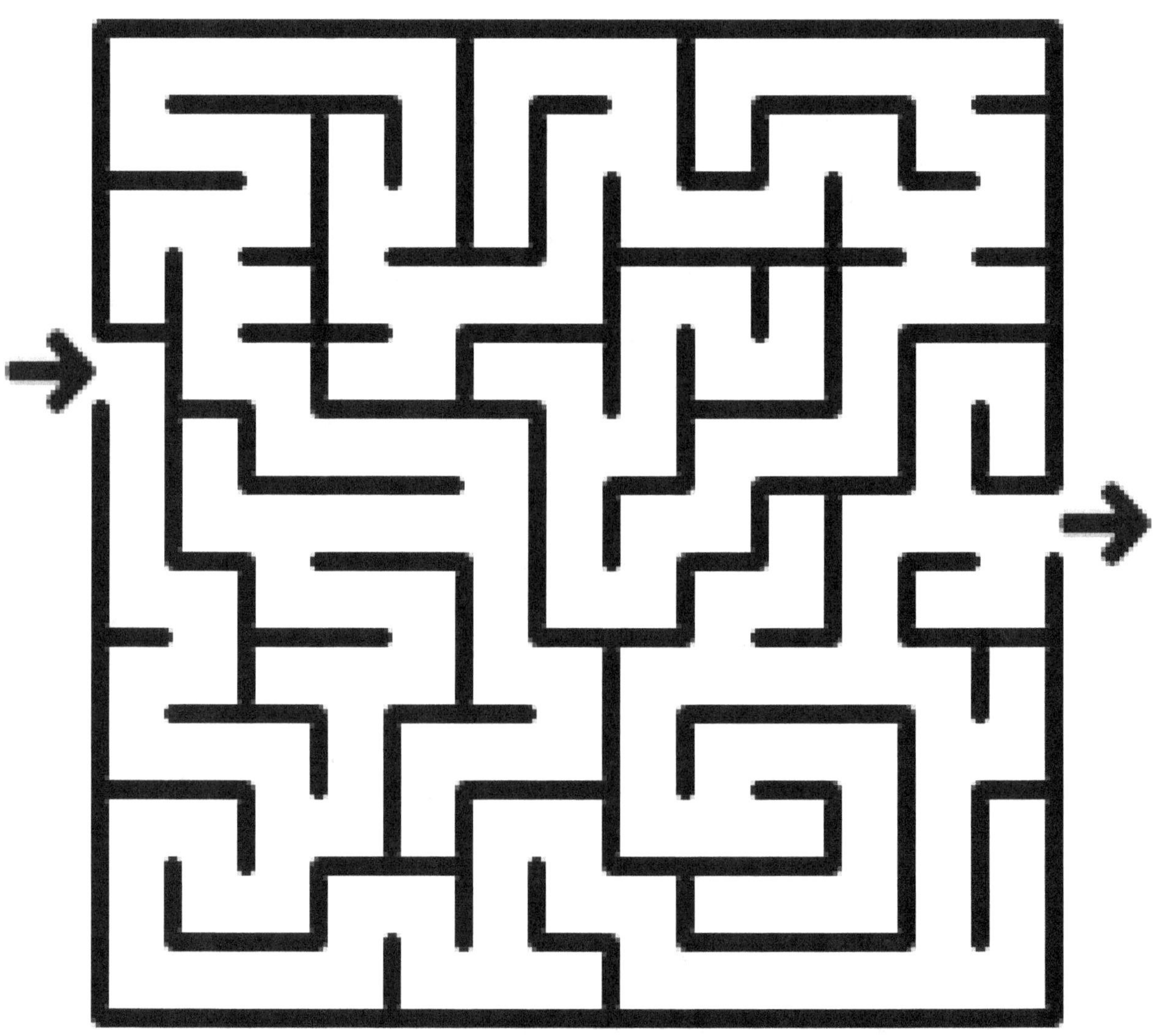

49
DIFFICULT

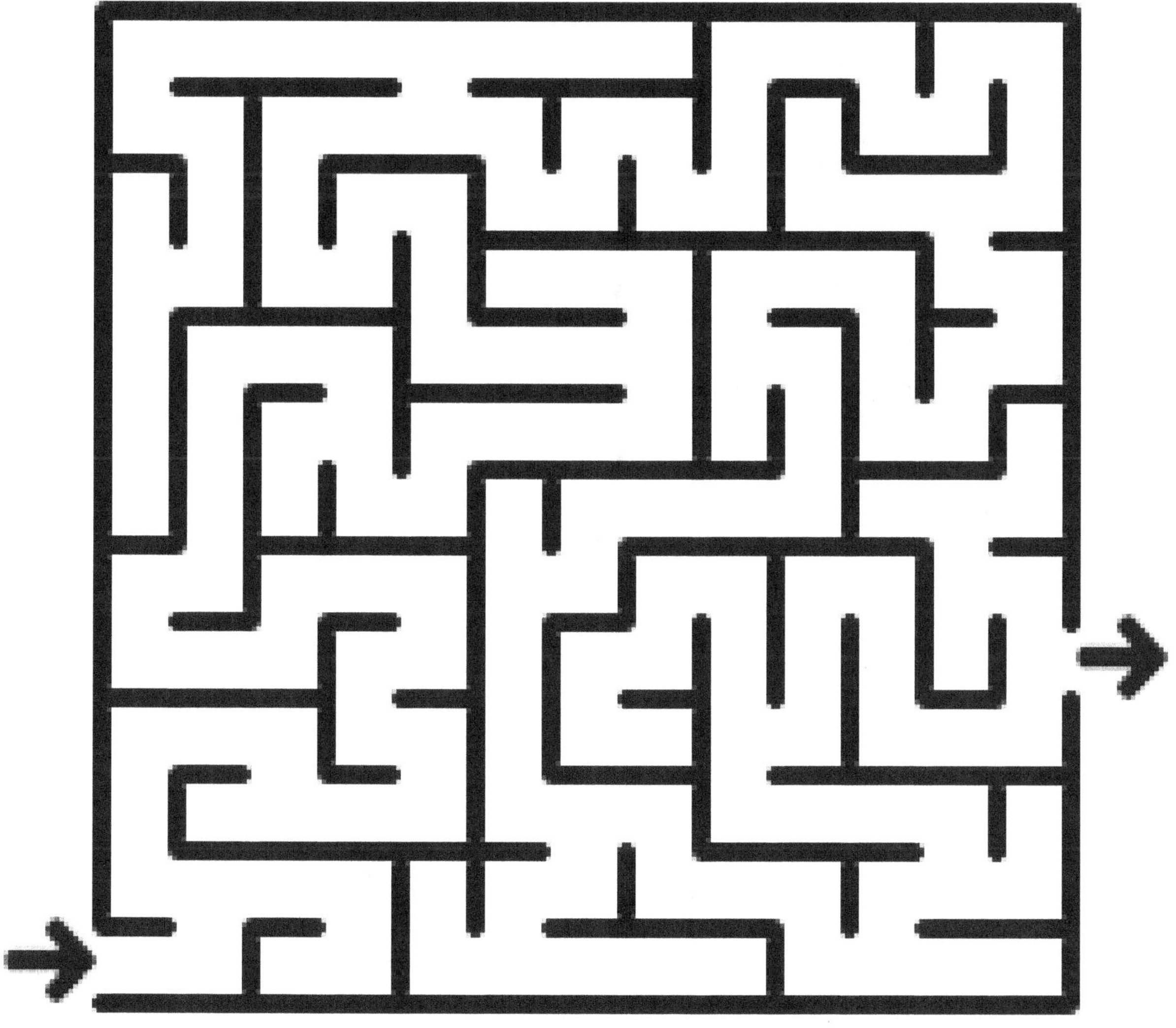

50
DIFFICULT

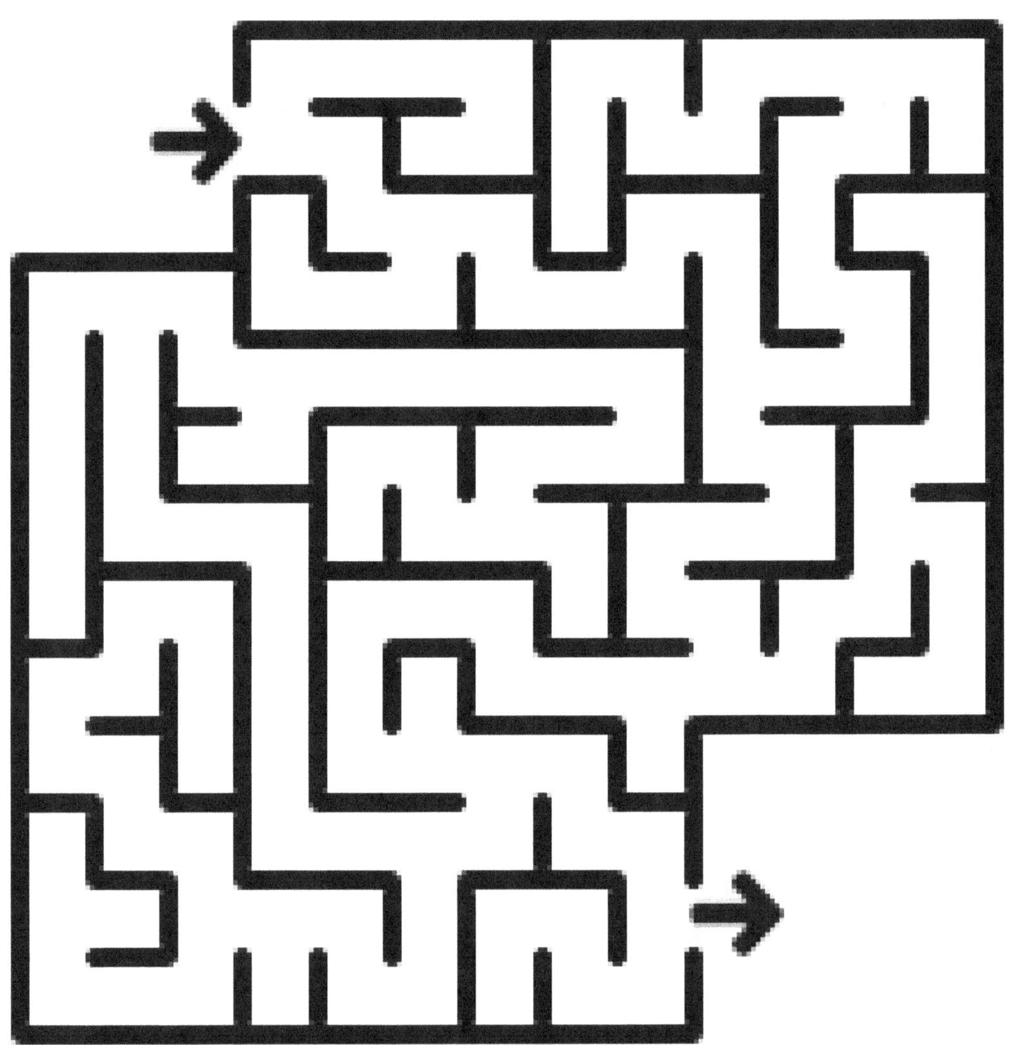

51
DIFFICULT

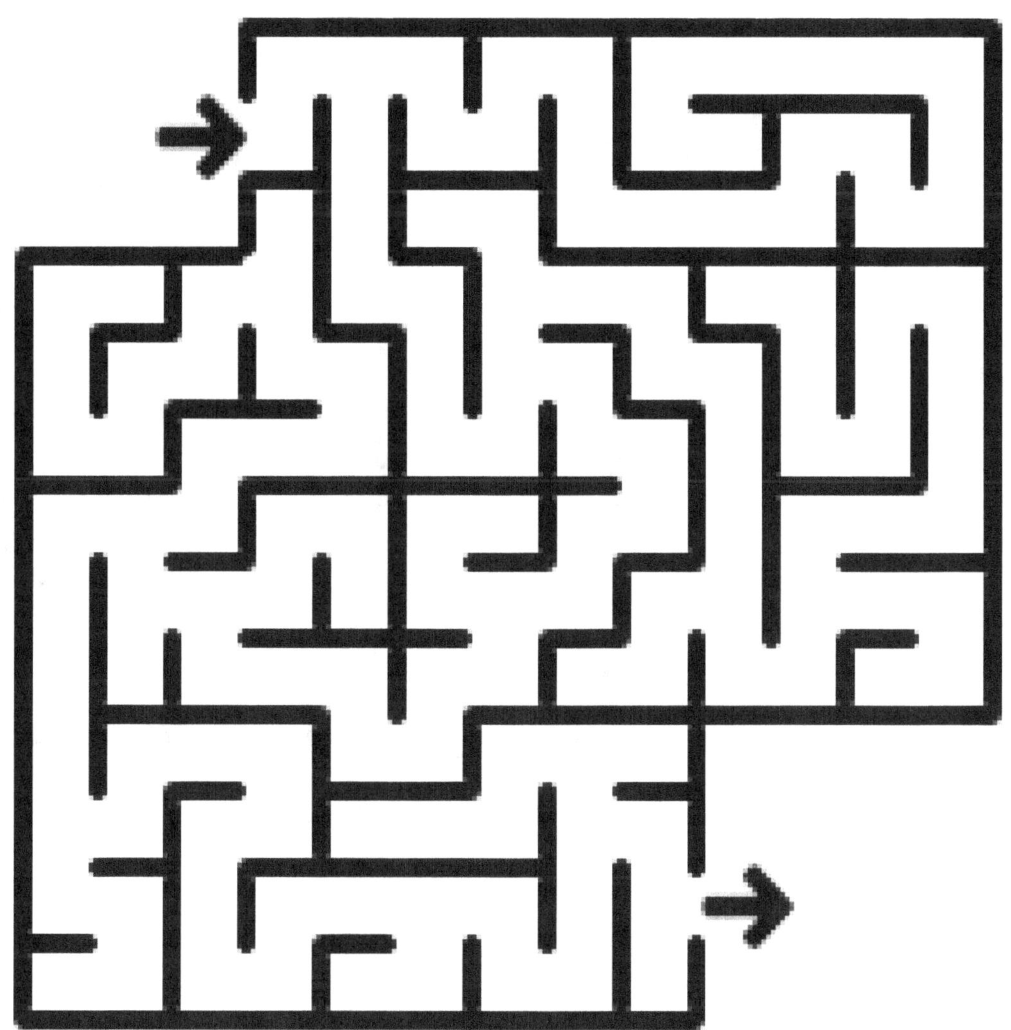

52
DIFFICULT

53
DIFFICULT

54
DIFFICULT

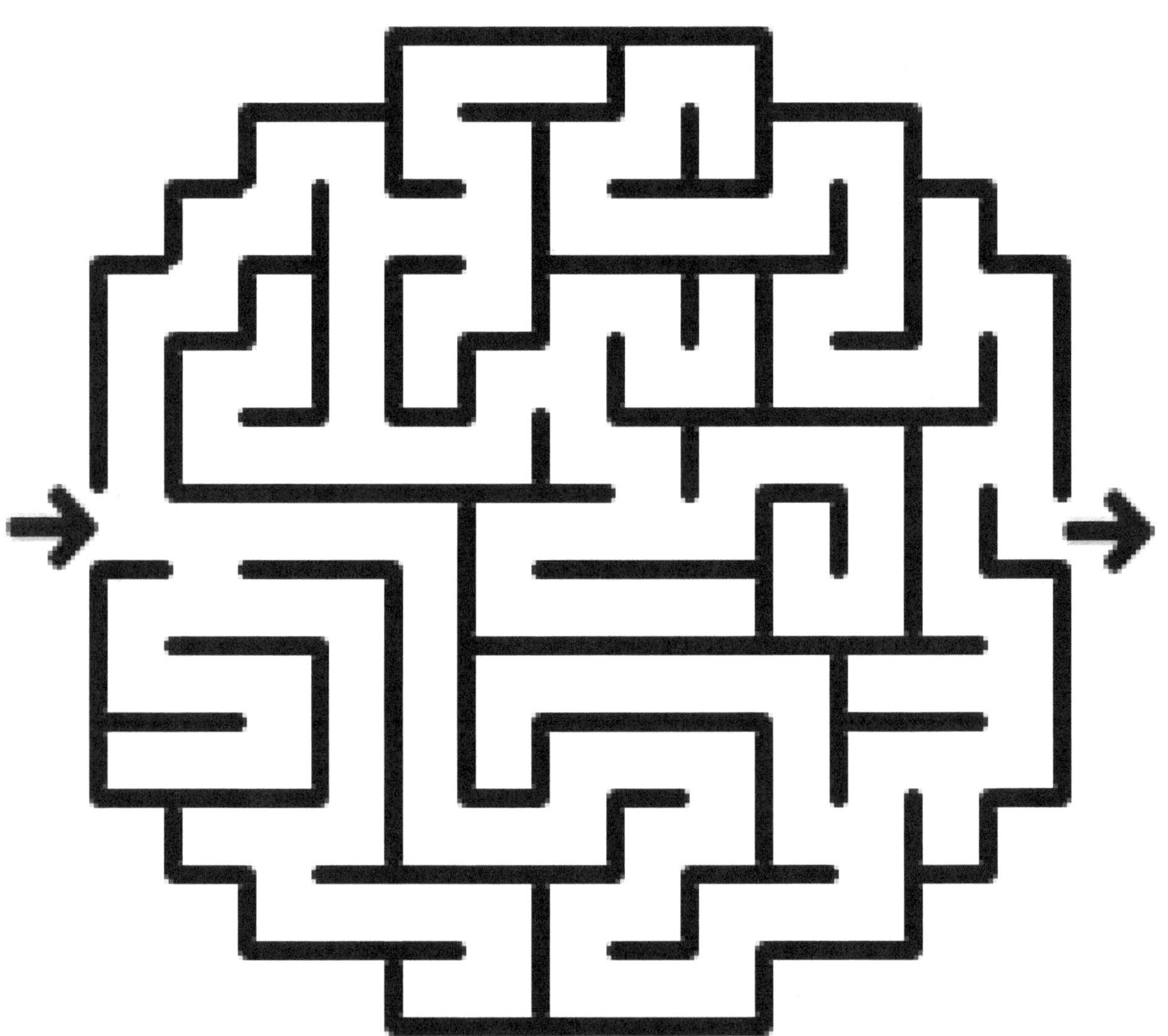

55
DIFFICULT

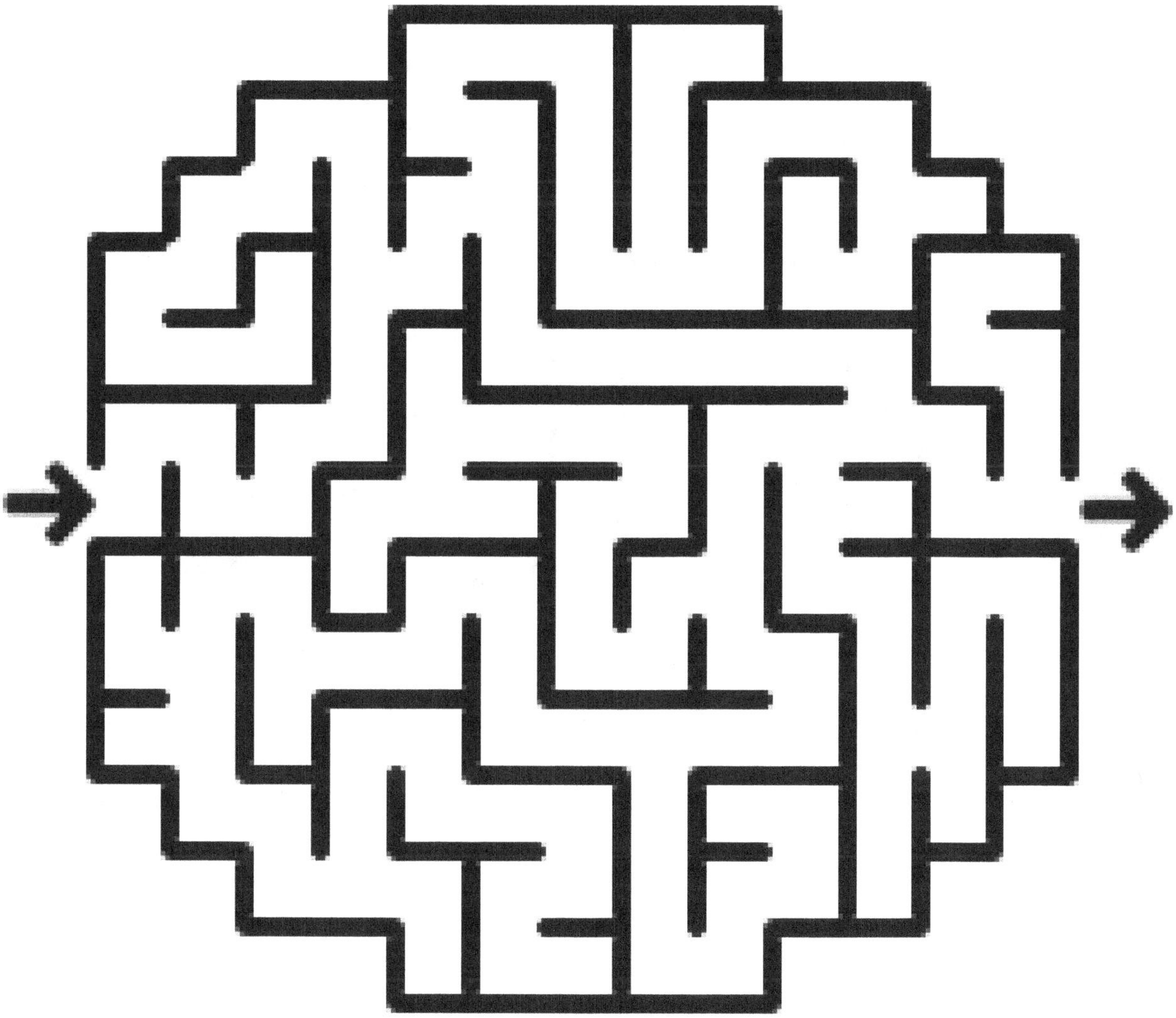

56
DIFFICULT

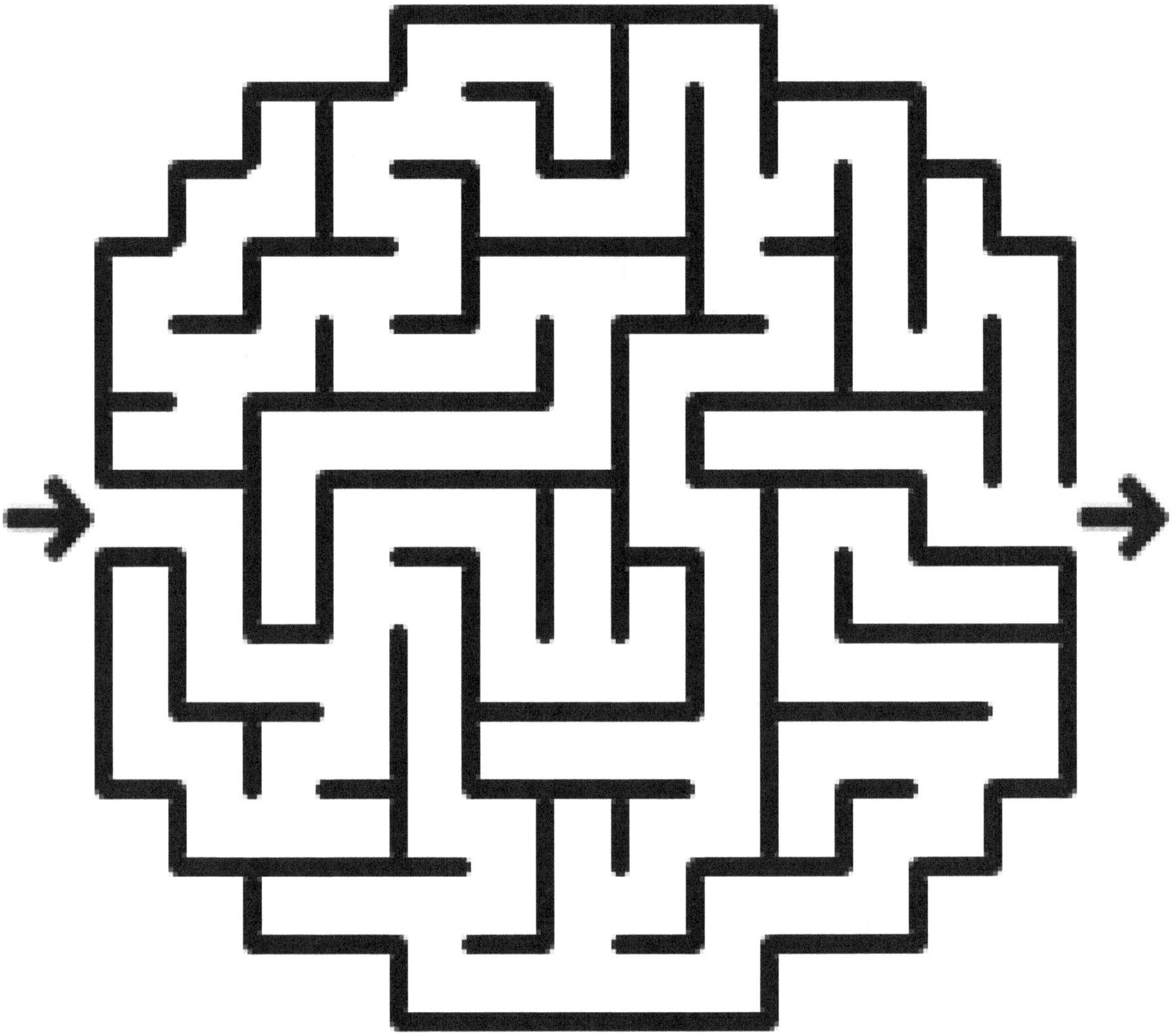

57
DIFFICULT

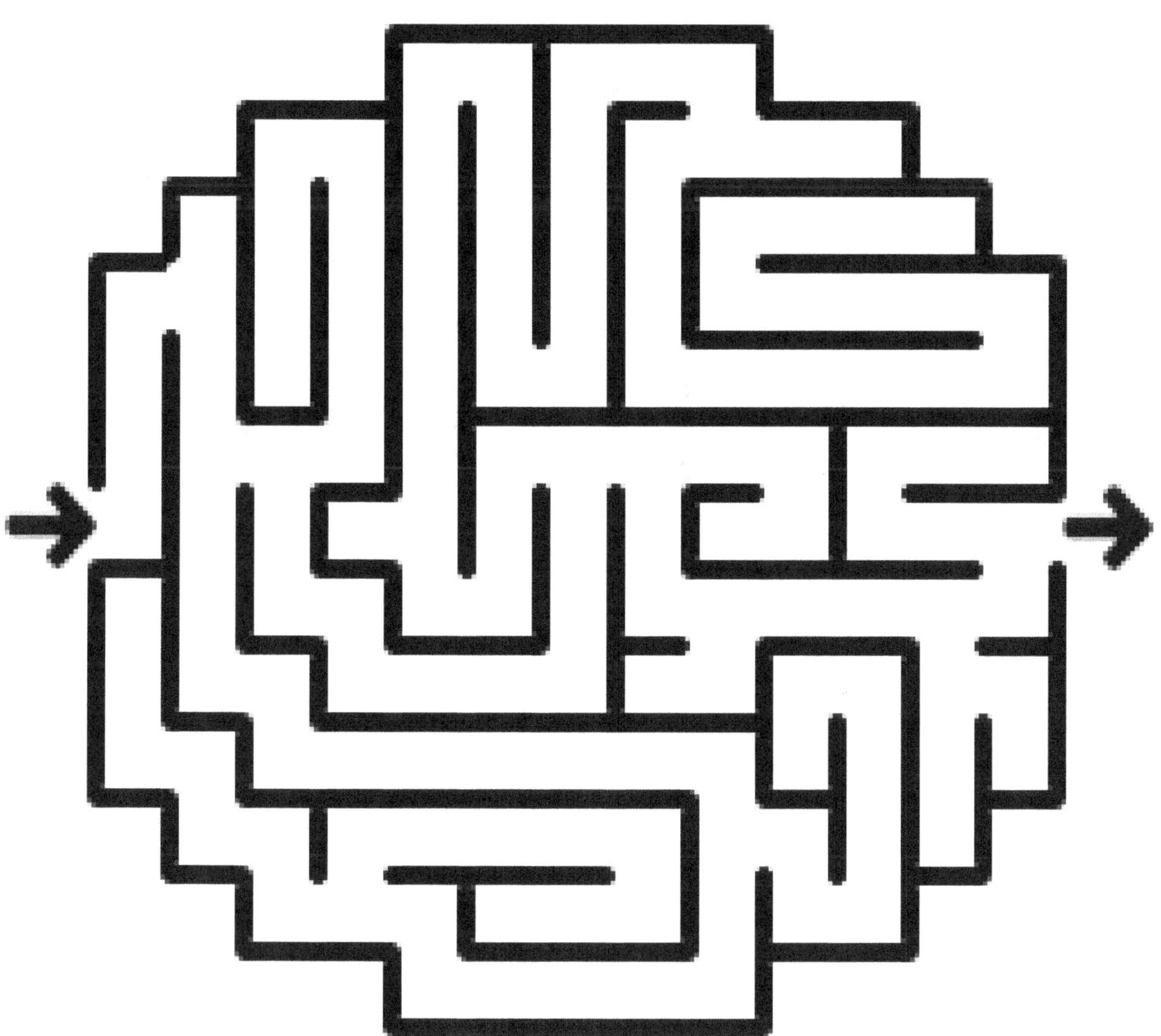

58
DIFFICULT

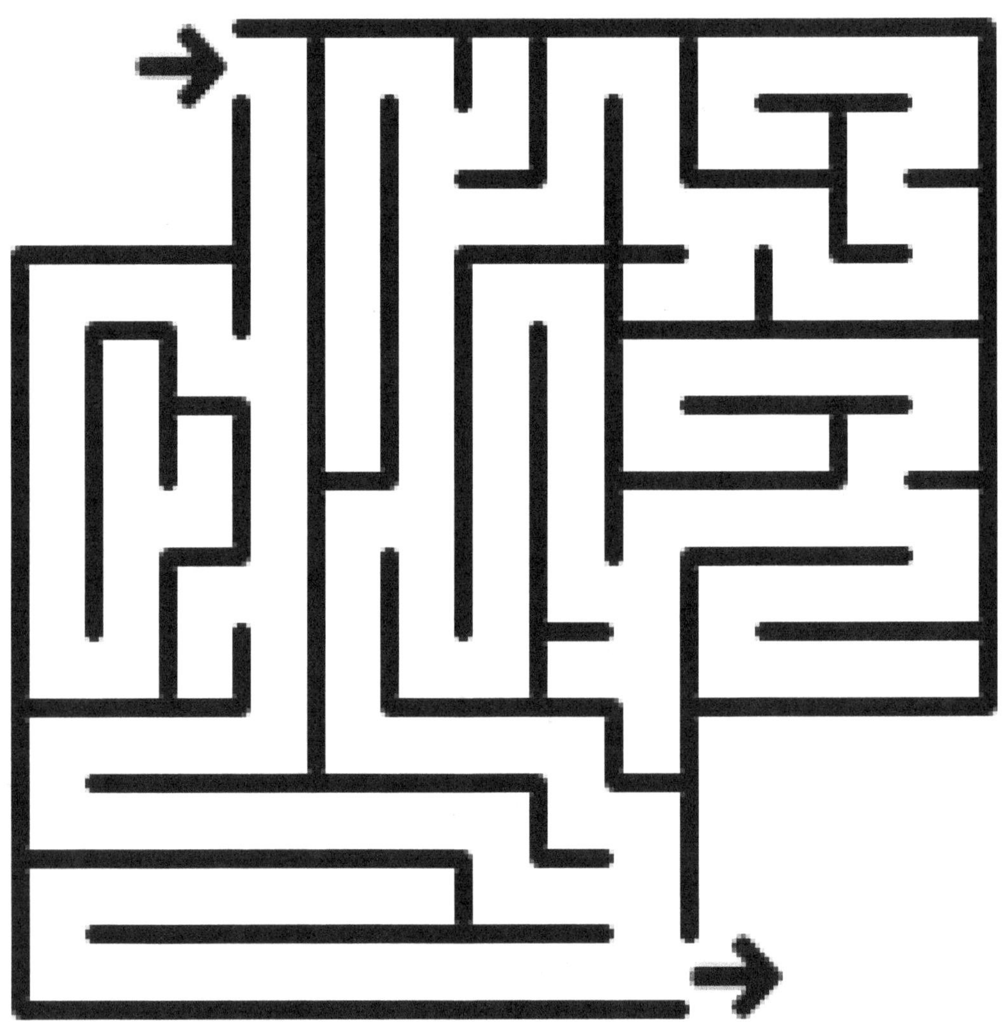

59
DIFFICULT

60
DIFFICULT

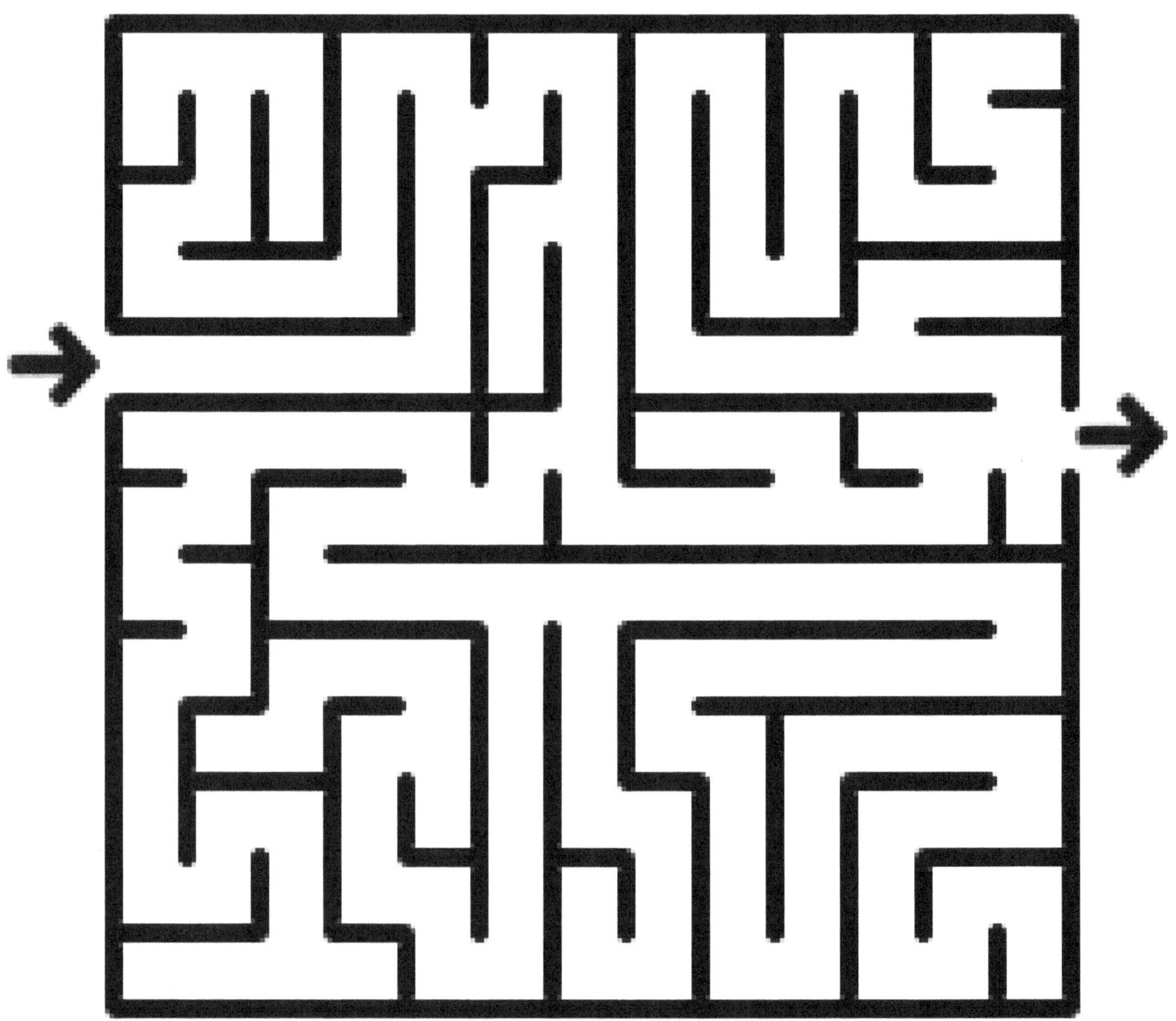

61
SUPER DIFFICULT

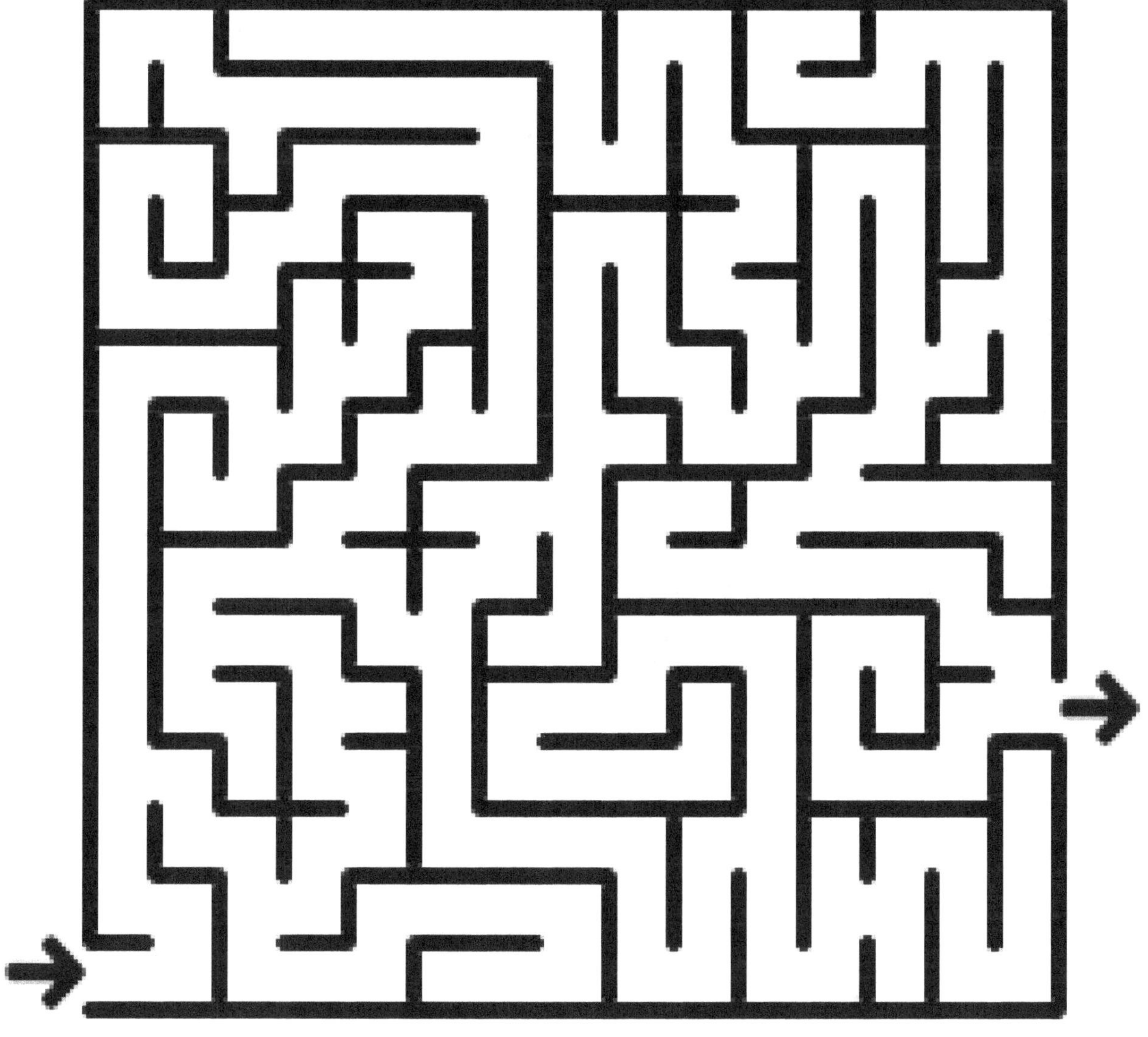

62
SUPER DIFFICULT

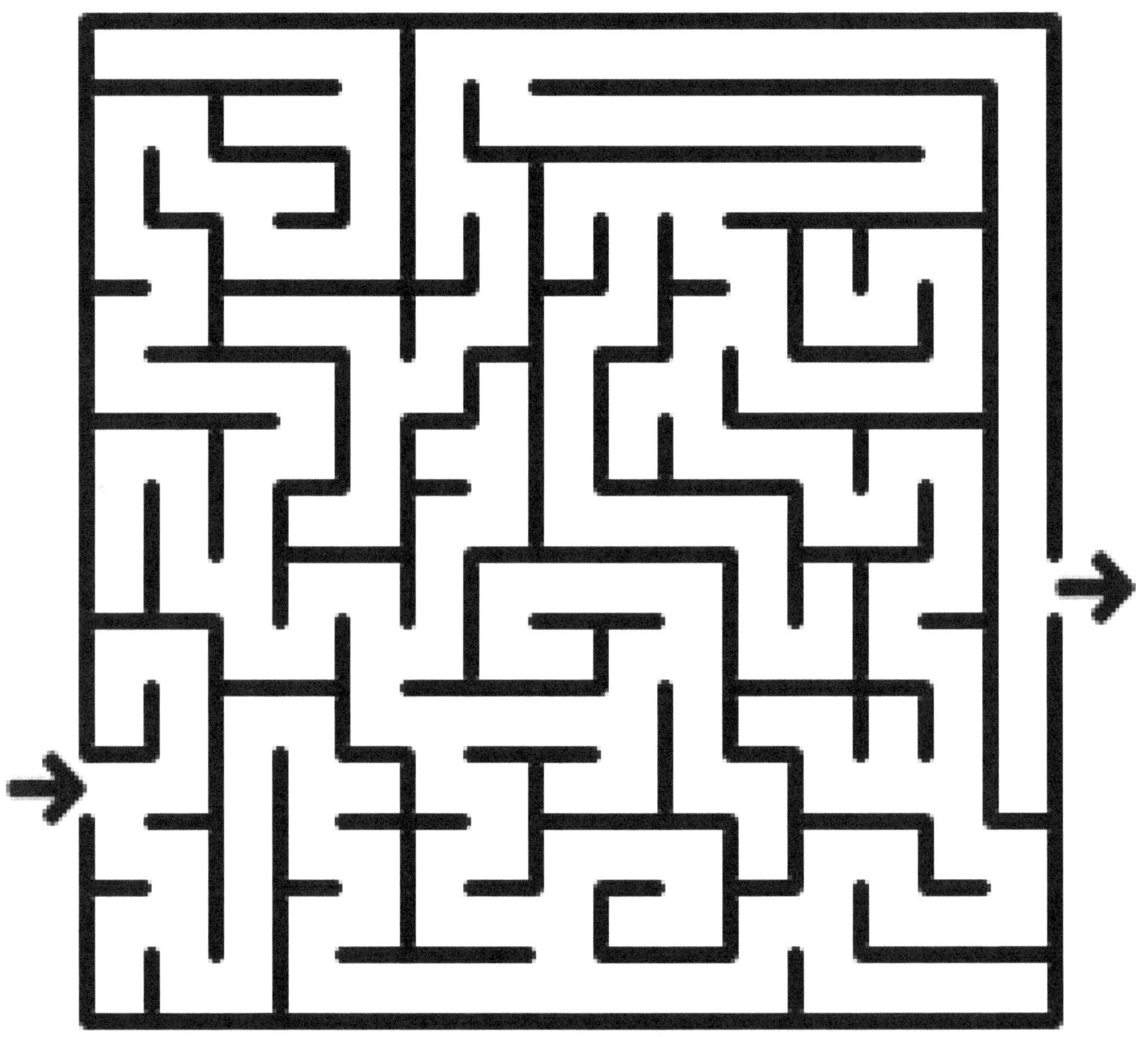

63
SUPER DIFFICULT

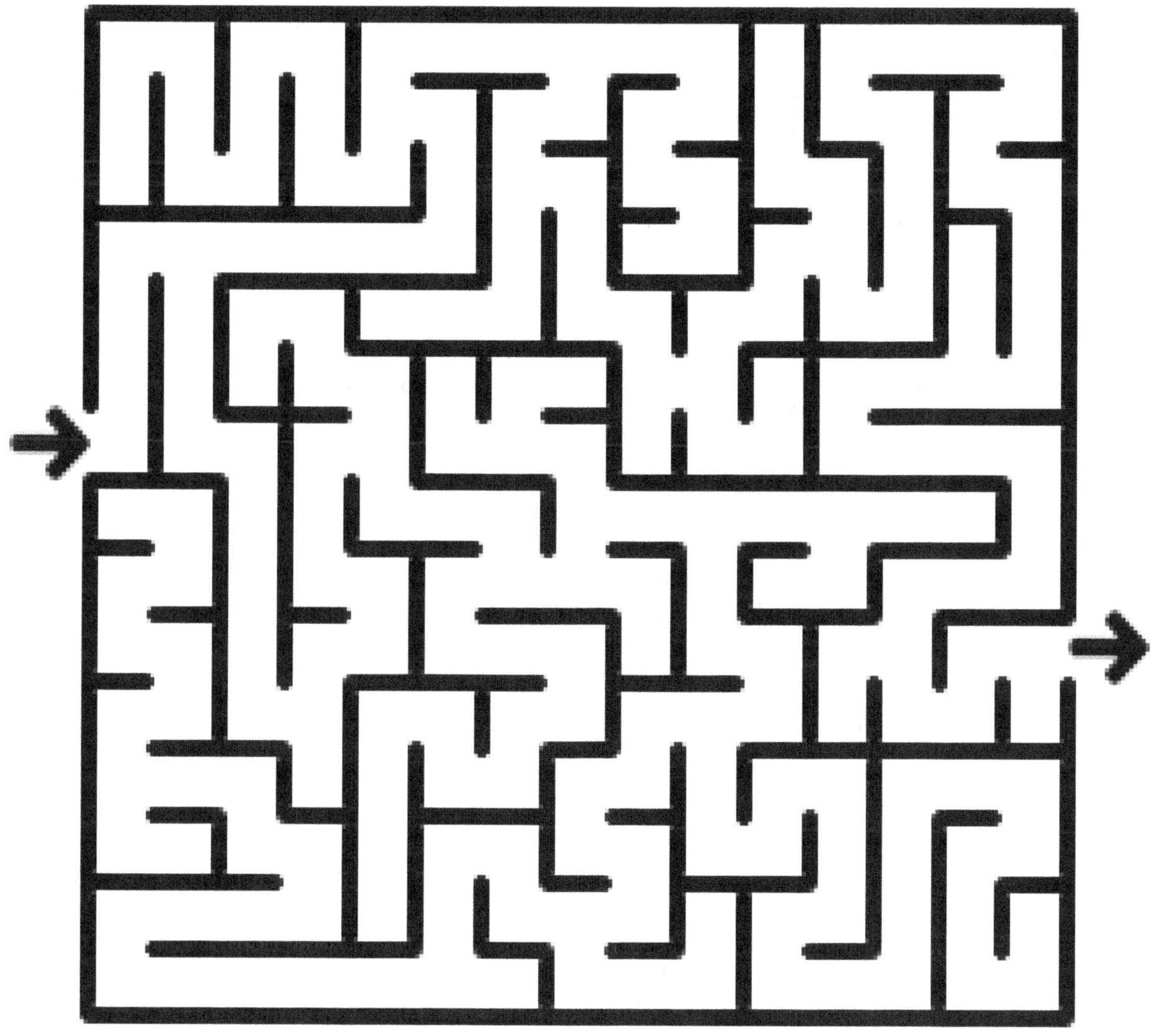

64
SUPER DIFFICULT

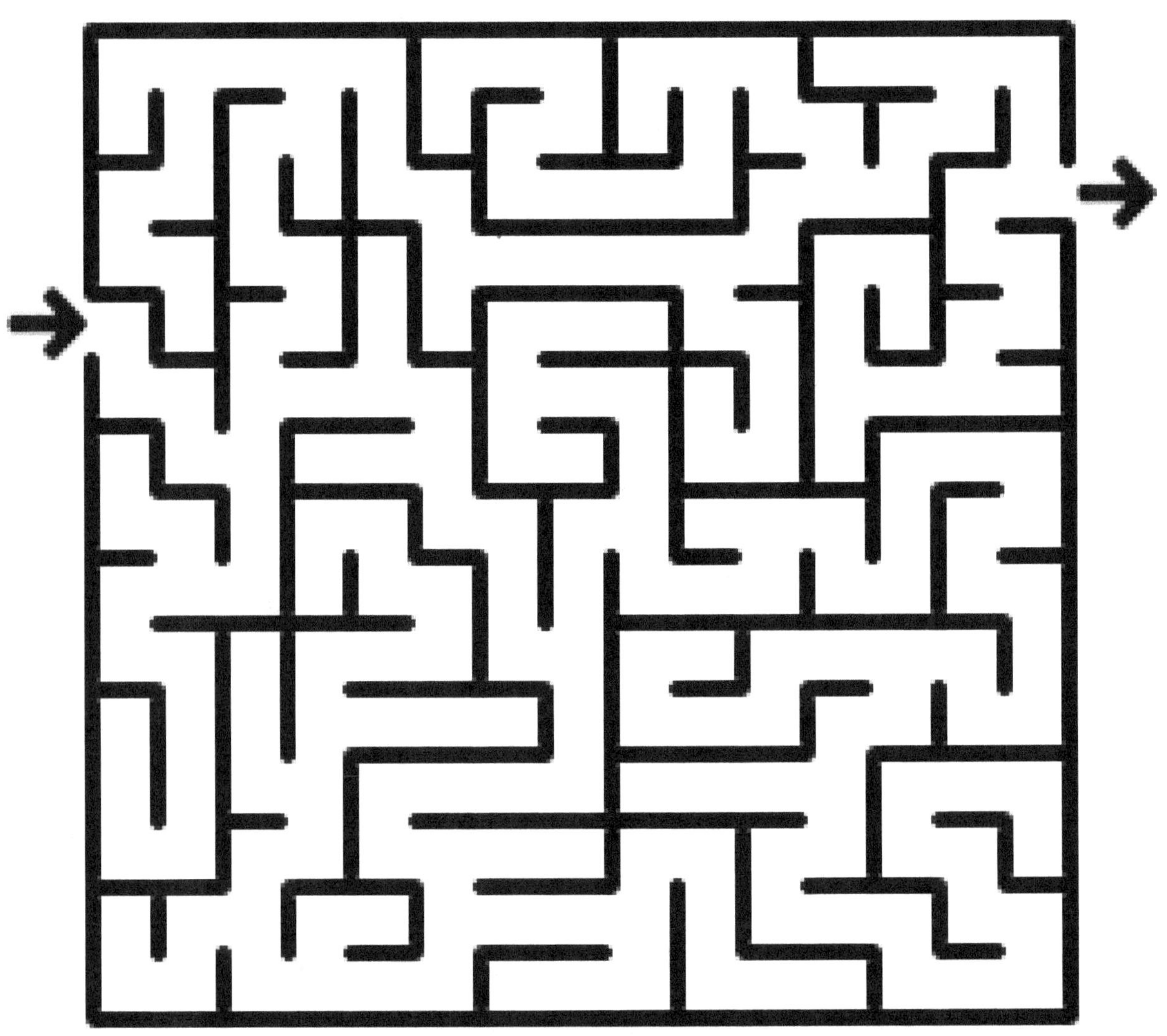

65
SUPER DIFFICULT

66
SUPER DIFFICULT

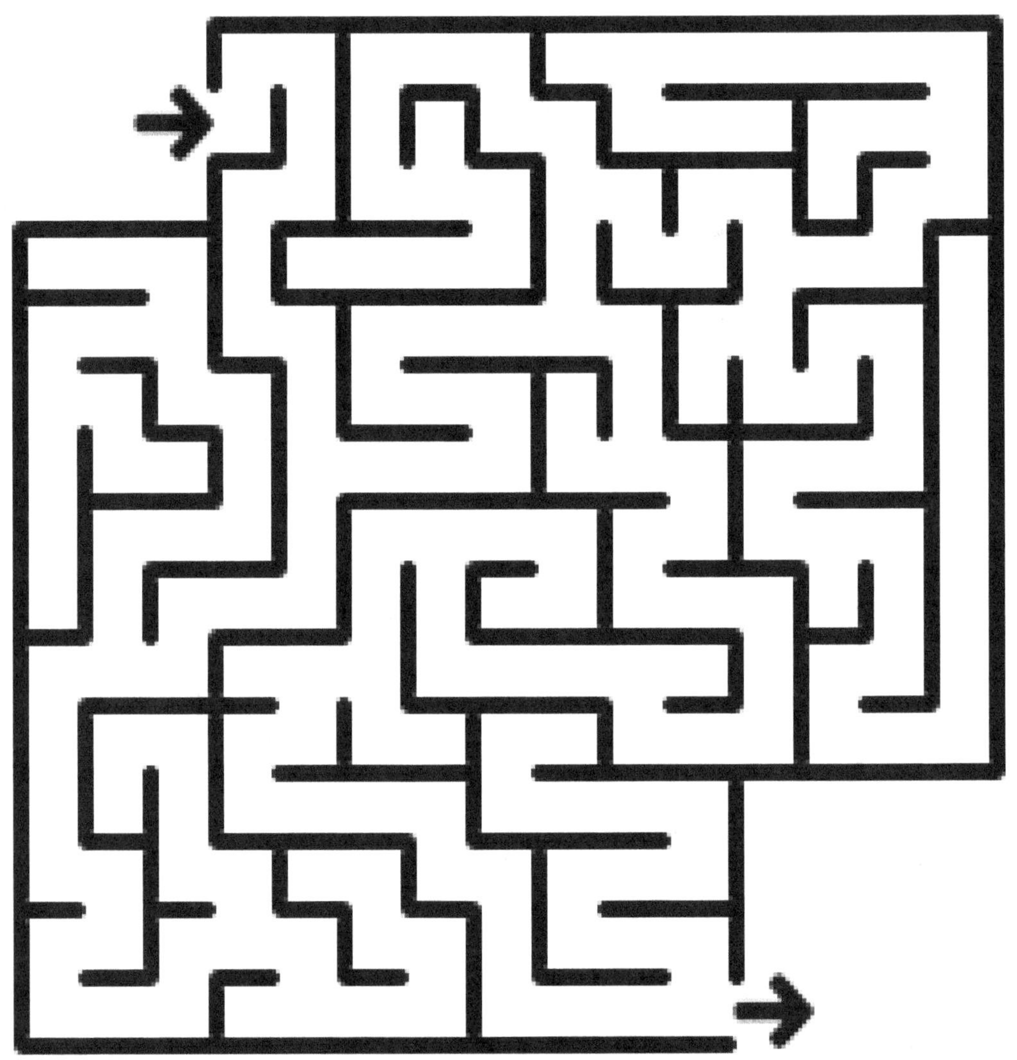

67
SUPER DIFFICULT

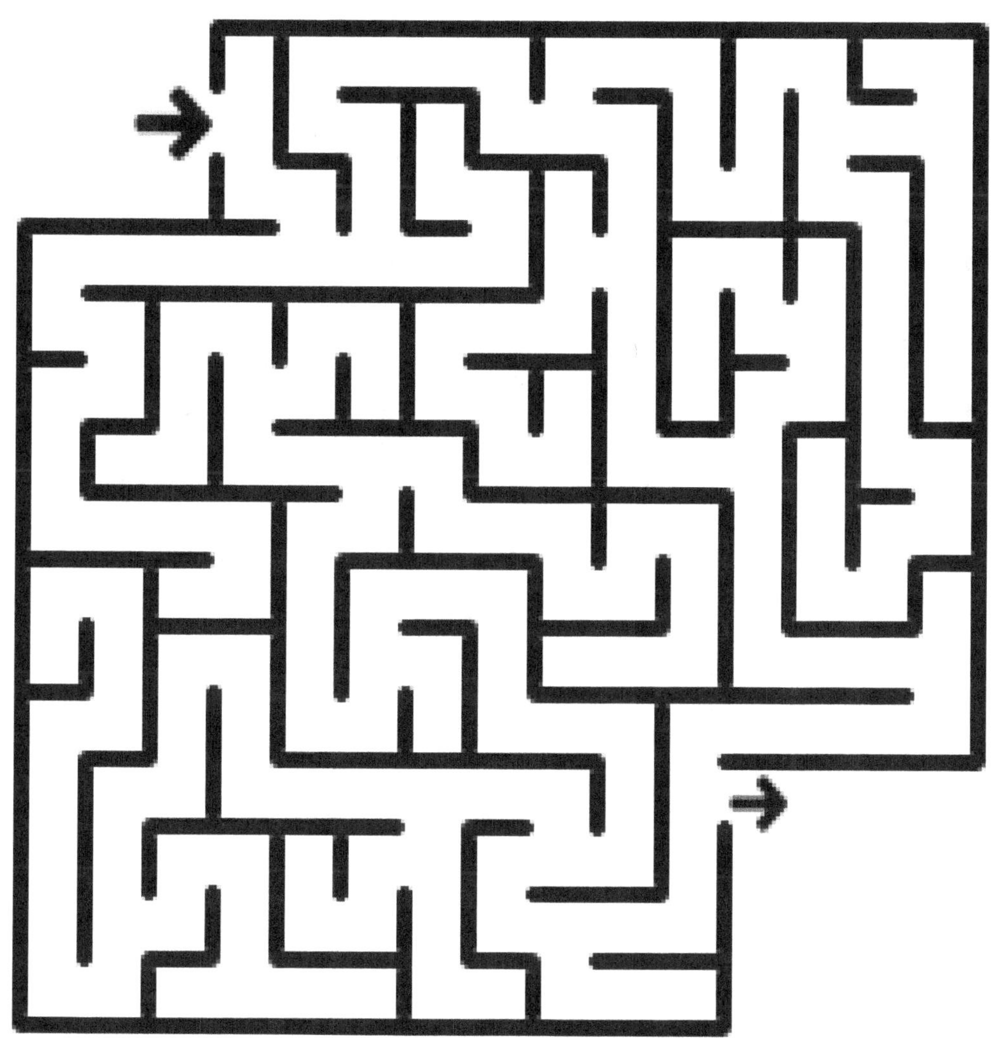

68
SUPER DIFFICULT

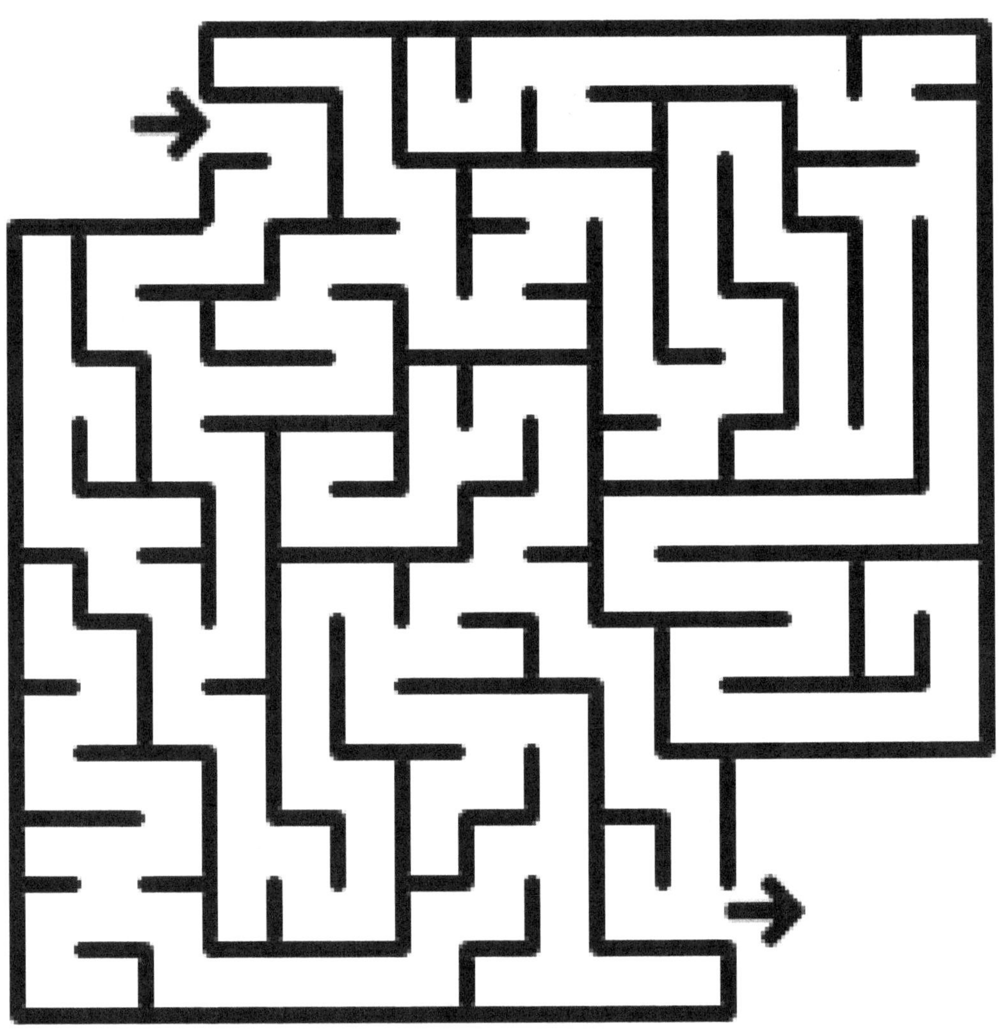

69
SUPER DIFFICULT

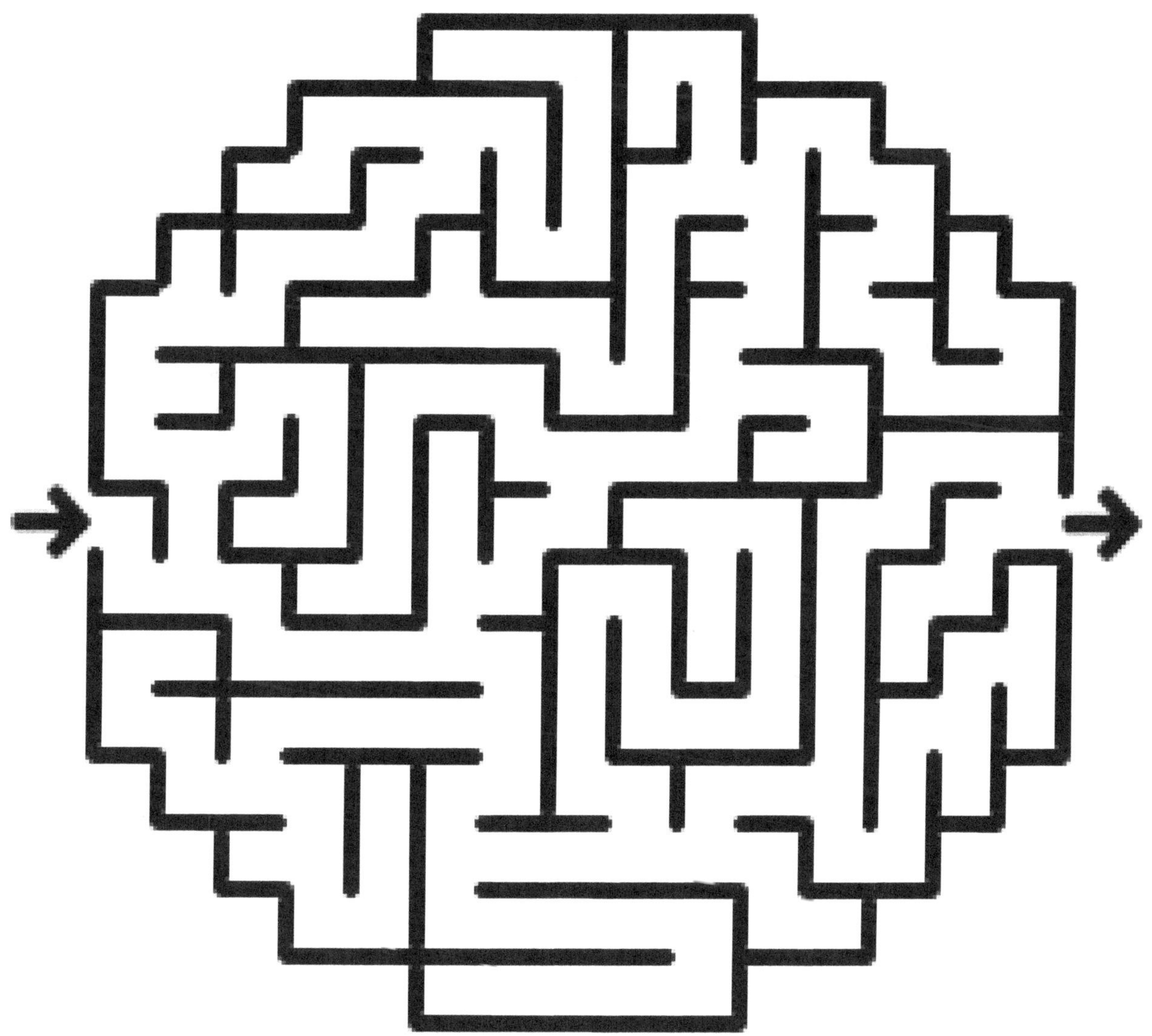

70
SUPER DIFFICULT

71
SUPER DIFFICULT

72
SUPER DIFFICULT

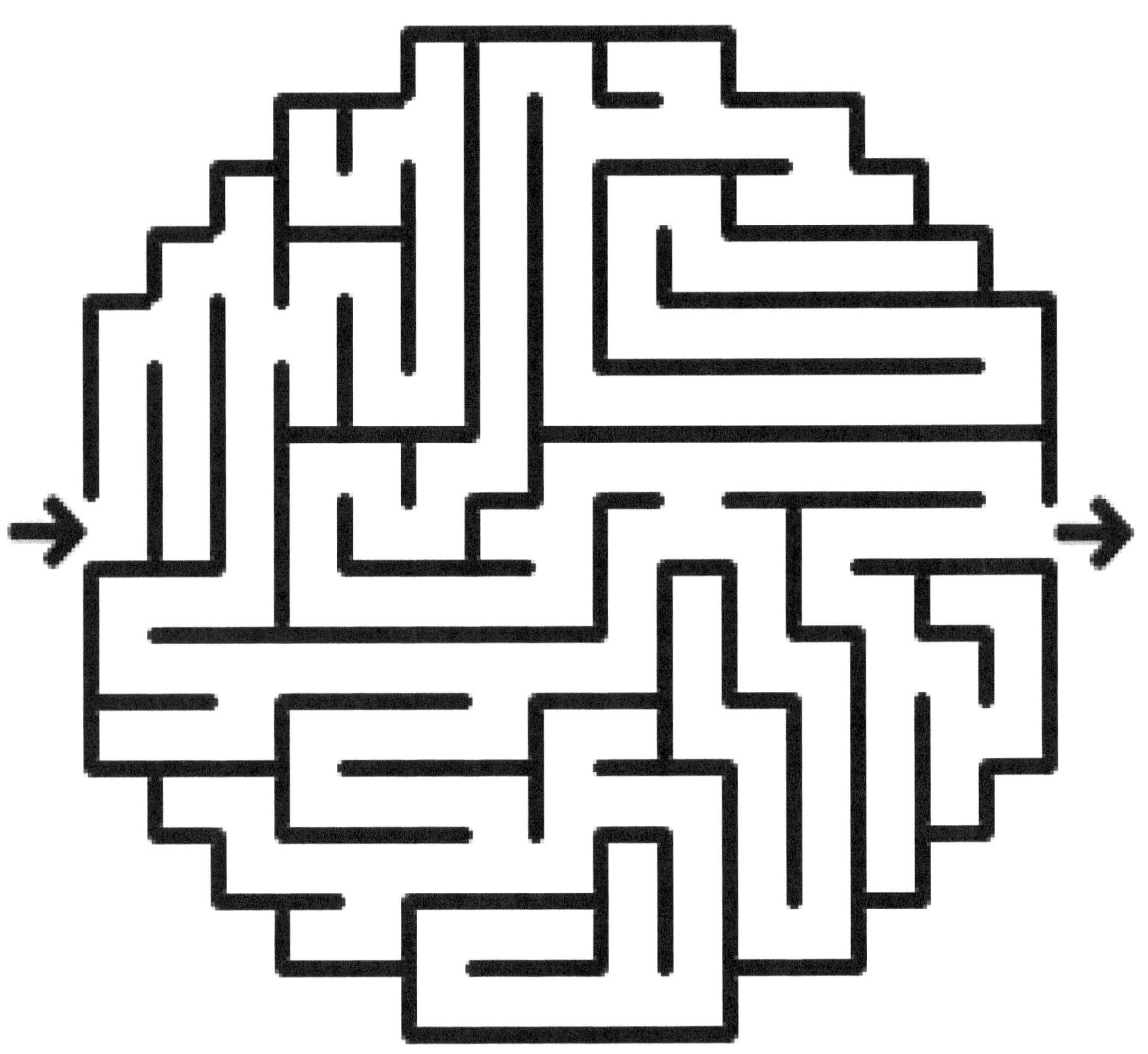

73
SUPER DIFFICULT

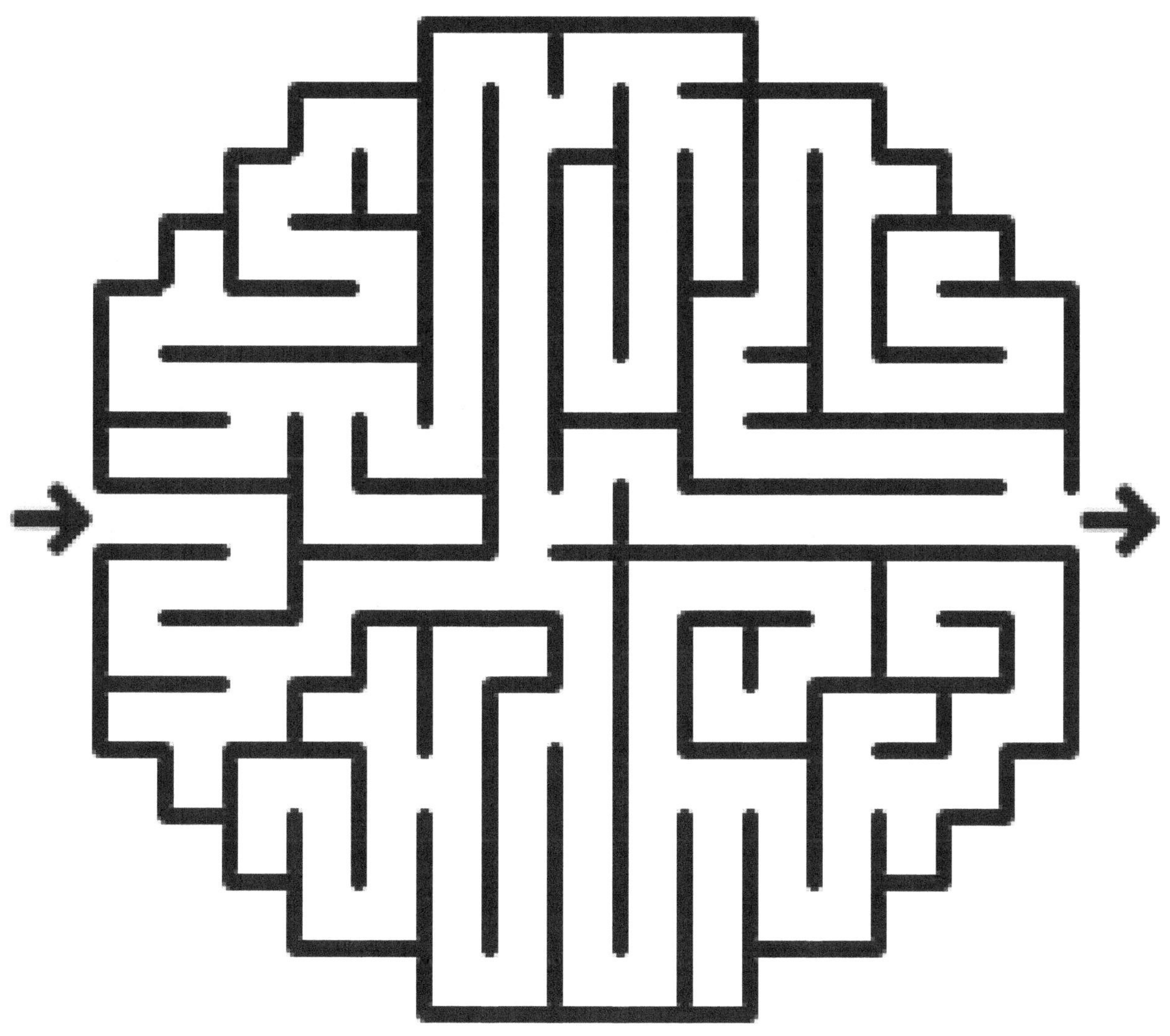

74
SUPER DIFFICULT

75
SUPER DIFFICULT

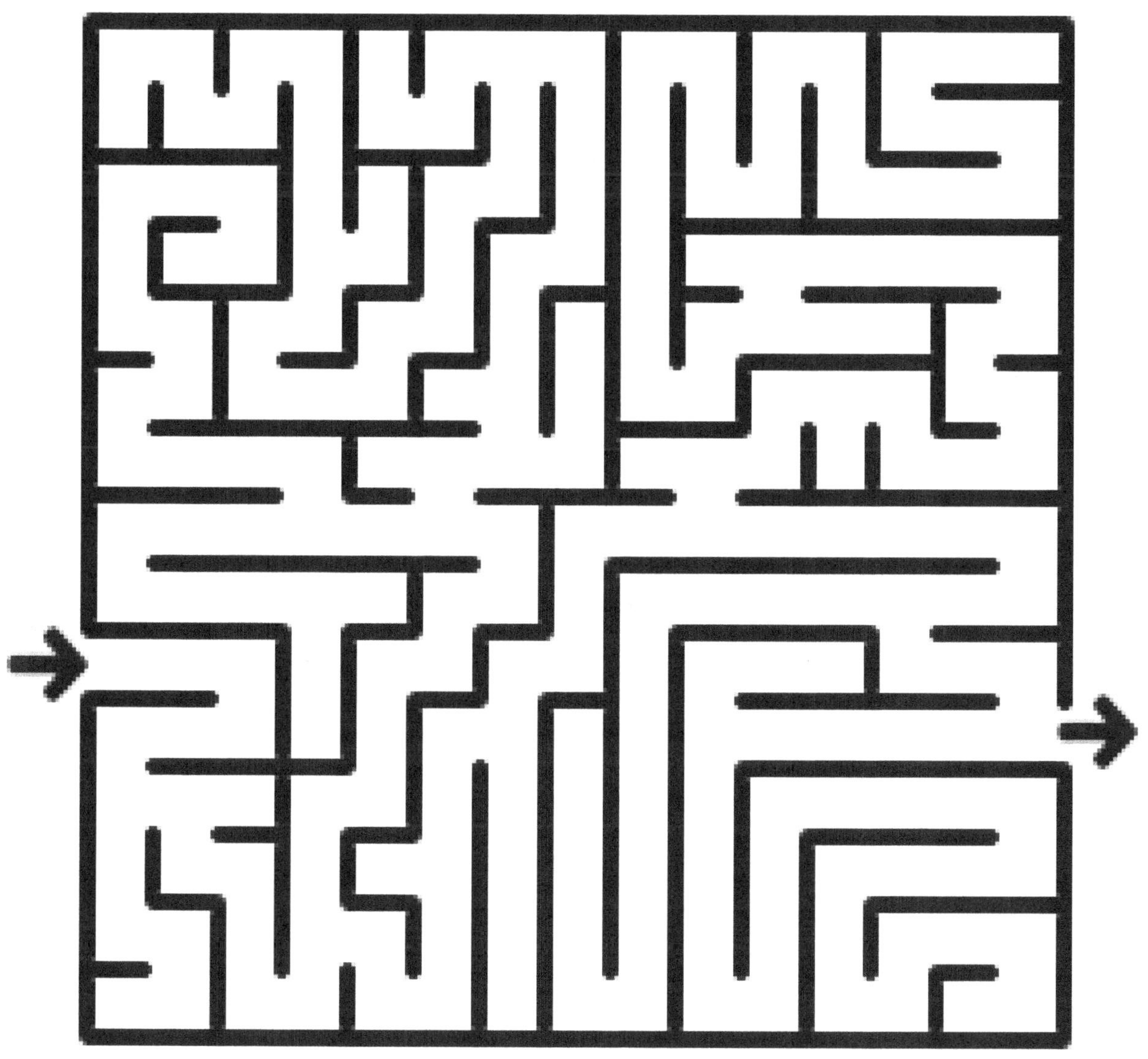

Name: ________________________________

Age: ________________________________

Notes

Name: _______________________________

Age: _______________________________

Notes

____

____

____

____

____

____

____

____

____

____

____

Also Available by the Same Authors:

Level 1
Kindergarten
Puzzles
Ages 4 - 8
Simple Puzzles
A
B
C
D
Worksheets
1
2
3
4
Activities for Kids
Peter I. Kattan
Nicola I. Kattan

Level 2
Kindergarten
Puzzles
Ages 4 - 8
Simple Puzzles
O
P
Q
R
Worksheets
6
7
8
9
Activities for Kids
Peter I. Kattan
Nicola I. Kattan

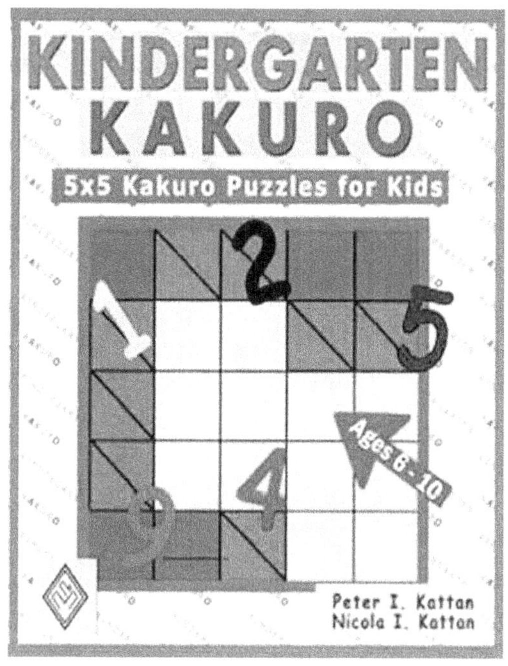

KINDERGARTEN
KAKURO
5x5 Kakuro Puzzles for Kids
Ages 6-10
Peter I. Kattan
Nicola I. Kattan

Preschool
SUDOKU
2x2 and 4x4
Sudoku Puzzles
for Kids
Includes
48
Puzzles
Ages
3-5 years
and up
PETRA
BOOKS

4x4 Sudoku Puzzles for Kids
Includes 80 Puzzles
KINDERGARTEN
SUDOKU
Ages 4 - 8 years and up
Peter I. Kattan
Nicola I. Kattan
PETRA BOOKS

MORE
KINDERGARTEN
SUDOKU
Ages 4 - 8 years and up
EASY
MEDIUM
DIFFICULT
4x4 Classic Sudoku Puzzles for Kids
Includes 96 Puzzles
Peter I. Kattan
Nicola I. Kattan

Simple Mazes for Children
75 Mazes with Five Levels of Difficulty for Kids

Simple Mazes for Children
75 Mazes with Five Levels of Difficulty for Kids